Embracing the Light

Achieving Spiritual Integration

Embracing The Light

Achieving
Spiritual Integration

---

by Robert R. Leichtman, M.D.
& Carl Japikse

ARIEL PRESS
Atlanta – Columbus

EMBRACING THE LIGHT
Copyright © 2005 by Light

ISBN 0-89804-173-2

Table of Contents

An Agent of Light   7

1. An Introduction to Spiritual Integration   17

2. Obstacles to Integration   29

3. The Basis for Integration   41

4. The Tools of Integration   52

5. Integrating Conduct with Intentions   64

6. Integrating the Emotions with the Mind   74

7. Integrating Ideas with Ideals   86

8. Integrating the Body with Its Purpose   98

9. Integrating Physical Events with Our
    Spiritual Destiny   109

10. Integrating Conflict with Spiritual Growth   121

11. Integrating Opportunities to Act with
    Cycles of Time   134

12. Integrating Patterns from the Past with
    Spiritual Potential   146

13. Integrating the Personality with the Soul   158

14. Integrating with Groups   170

To

All Members

of Light

Past, Present, and Future

Introduction

An Agent
of Light

The path to enlightenment begins with an understanding—the understanding that we are a being of light. We possess, on loan, bodies of flesh, feeling, and thought, but these are only temporary residences. The real home of our selfhood is a body of light. Our bodies of flesh, feeling, and thought serve their function, and then they pass, but our true nature in light does not pass. Neither does it fail.

We are made as spirit; spirit is the cause of our being and all which happens to us. This spirit is a spark of divine energy; as it seeks expression as an individual, the spark glows and radiates, producing light. This is not physical light, which is feeble and dim, but the light of consciousness: immortal, unlimited, and creative. It is the substance of our humanity, the wellspring of our individuality, talent, wisdom, love, courage, and joy.

It is important to recognize this inner nature of light and distinguish it from the form and activity of the personality. Since we are a being of light, we ought to be inspired by this light, motivated by this light, and healed by this light. Yet often we are not.

The problem is one of becoming aware of our true identity. Through many eons, the light—which is our true self—has projected its radiance into the shadows of form, seeking to illumine that which is obscured. In the process, however, our personal sense of identity, which should be filled with light, has been blurred; we have identified with the shadows. We have come to think of ourself in terms of our experiences, perceptions, reactions, hurts, achievements, and associations—instead of as light. The poet Robert Frost captures this dilemma poignantly:

> I have been one acquainted with the night.
> I have walked out in rain—and back in rain.
> I have outwalked the furthest city light.
> I have looked down the saddest city lane.
> I have passed by the watchman on his beat
> And dropped my eyes, unwilling to explain.

To properly honor the light within us, we must look beyond the night. We must renew our acquaintance with light. Primarily, this means identifying with the soul and its plans, rather than the personality, with its wants, complaints, and difficulties.

An analogy which helps illustrate why this is important is the nature of physical light as it expresses itself through a light bulb. The bulb is the form through which the light shines, and yet it is not light. Nor can it produce light by itself. Only when it is connected to a source of electricity can the light bulb actually give off light.

Unless connected with spirit, our personality is no better able to produce the light it is designed to express than a light bulb that is not connected with electricity. Enlightenment is never produced in the personality alone; it is the result of integrating the daily life of the personality with the purposes and life of spirit.

It is this dynamic interplay which causes the light of our being to shine in the physical world.

Enlightenment has little to do with being able to see white light, "open the third eye," or run white light energy up and down the spine. Instead, the enlightened individual is one who is focused in the light of the soul and is able to sustain that focus through his daily self-expression. The hallmarks of enlightenment are mastery of the emotions, the ability to comprehend the "mysteries" of life, and the capacity to work creatively in life.

It should be obvious, therefore, that the single most important step toward enlightenment is the effort to make the personality a more fit vehicle for the light of God. Enlightenment is the product primarily of the effort to express our talent, wisdom, love, courage, and joy as fully as possible in our daily activities. Or, to put this idea a little more poetically, enlightenment is achieved by learning to breathe in and breathe out the light of the soul. We breathe in the light by attuning ourself to the ideals of life and filling our awareness, our appreciation, and our adoration with these ideals. We breathe out the light by seeking to invest these same ideals in all that we do—in our work, relationships, hobbies, and recreation.

In all these endeavors, our goal must be to unite the events and needs of the personality with the actual light of the soul. This involves four basic stages:

1. Discovering the light. It may be tempting to dismiss this stage of enlightenment as trivial, but it is not. Long after the personality intellectually and emotionally recognizes that there is a soul and its nature is light, it still insists on substituting something less than real in lieu of light. In confronting a difficult relationship, for example, the personality may go through the motions of consulting the soul as to how to proceed—and then block out the light and do what it prefers anyway. And yet the self-deception is accepted; the personality contentedly believes it is fulfilling the desires of the soul, even while gratifying its own wishes and whims.

To *discover* the light, therefore, we must begin by distinguishing between light and shadow. Light impels us to grow. It leads us into paths of rightness. It causes us to increase our skills, our understanding, and our compassion. It is found in our highest aspirations, ideals, values, and maturity—never in our wishes and good feelings.

2. Comprehending the light. Once the light is discovered, it must be understood and rightly interpreted. This stage is not an easy one to master, as light is multidimensional by nature. It cannot be understood only in three-dimensional terms; the study of light forces us to think in terms of immortality and infinity as well. It forces us to give up one limitation of thought after another.

Understanding the nature of our personal destiny is a good example of this difficulty. It frequently occurs that certain events befall us that make little sense in the context of our work, needs, or other activities. The personality is often confused by these events, and may even question the wisdom of a soul which could let them happen. It may doubt the benevolence of the light itself. Such doubts and puzzlements, however, are simply signs of incomprehension. The vastness of light has escaped our narrow view. Inevitably, such circumstances *do* fit a larger pattern of continuity, either helping us learn a lesson we have been studiously ignoring for a long time, or preparing us for opportunities as yet unseen in the shadows of daily life—but perfectly obvious in the light of spirit.

Another instance of the difficulty of comprehending the light is in the difference between the conventional expressions of the ideals of love, joy, beauty, and wisdom and their actual realities in light. All too often, for example, the expression of love is marred by sentimentality, possessiveness, and jealousy. Enlightened love, however, has nothing to do with these distortions.

Thus, to *comprehend* light, we must seek always to look for the higher perspective which makes sense of our feelings, attitudes, challenges, and conflicts. When light is properly comprehended, it removes all doubt, second-guessing, and confusion.

3. Integrating the light. At the level of the soul, we are a being of light, but the personality remains in shadow. The third stage of enlightenment, consequently, is the integration of the light of the soul with the needs and activities of the personality, so that our daily self-expression radiates light as well. In practical terms, this means blending the light of our love, joy, courage, and wisdom into the unredeemed or imperfect elements of our attitudes, habits, values, talents, and activities.

As the path to enlightenment is trod, the crabby, blighted, mean, and ignorant areas of our personality slowly ebb away, and are replaced by light. We treat others better than before. We view ourself with more dignity; we act with a greater measure of gracefulness. We eliminate our tendencies toward carelessness, dishonesty, and laziness. In this way, we become a more effective person, by ridding ourself of that which does not embody the light.

This is not a matter of accommodation, where we layer a thin icing of niceness over an otherwise hostile and selfish personality. As Jesus put it, "No one can serve two masters." It is not possible to serve the light and the shadow both; therefore, to *integrate* the light into the personality, we must remove all traces of shadow. We must purge that which is impure and welcome into our consciousness that which will honor the light. We must harmonize the personality with the plans and purposes of the soul.

4. Expressing the light. Again Jesus said, "Men do not light a lamp and put it under a bushel, but on a stand, so it gives light to all in the house. Let your light so shine before all men, that they may see your good works and give glory to your Father who is in heaven." The work of enlightenment is a private undertaking between the personality and the soul, but the fruits of enlightenment must be shared with all. Light is radiant; it is against its nature to be contained and held private. If we are not working to express light in all we do and think and say, we are not really dealing with light at all—just a glimmer.

We *express* the light by building, serving, and healing with it. Light seeks to create; as we become creative, even in humble ways, we express the light. Light seeks to serve; as we contribute to its service, we express the light. Light seeks to heal; as we focus its healing warmth, for the benefit of others, ourself, and civilization, we express the light.

Usually this creativity, serving, and healing is far from spectacular. It is carried out quietly, without fanfare, in the context of our work, relationships, interests, and social responsibilities. By striving to enlighten life and leave it a little better than we found it, we express light.

These four stages of the process of enlightenment apply not just to individuals, of course, but to the groups and institutions of humanity as well. Churches, governments, science, and civilization need enlightenment as well as individuals. So do education, literature, business, the arts, and other significant avenues of human endeavor. The same principles apply. Little is gained just by polishing up the shadowed forms of these institutions or enterprises, through the infusion of large amounts of money or worry. What is required is a genuine perception of the lighted ideal within these endeavors, a comprehension of how it can best be honored, hard work in harmonizing the group involved with the direction of light, and continued effort to express the highest measure of light possible.

If we persevere, the reward is great. We become an agent of light.

The lessons in the *Enlightenment* series all deal with this theme—becoming an agent of light. The intent is to demonstrate what it means to discover the light, comprehend it, integrate that light into the life of the personality, and express it in all we think, do, and say.

In their original form, the lessons of light were grouped in seven categories. Each lesson covered a topic from one specific category. This book, *Embracing the Light*, is a compilation of the fourteen lessons from *Enlightenment* that deal with the topic of spiritual integration and its pivotal role in the process of enlightenment. The other six categories present lessons that are also important to the development of the agent of light. These six categories are:

• The nature of psychic skills and awareness.

• Self-expression and why it is important, with lessons on the male/female principles, creativity, healing, the enlightened work ethic, and group expressions.

• Divine archetypes and how they express light through religion, mythology, literature, music, and the events of individual life.

• Enriching the mind—through reading, appreciation of the arts, interaction with the fourth and fifth dimensions, observation of life, and interpretation of dreams.

• The process of learning, and its importance to the life of spirit.

• Interacting with other kingdoms of life and discerning the value of their relationship with humanity, thereby expanding our awareness of the full scope of divine life.

Enlightenment is a call to action, not just fodder for further intellectual study. Becoming an agent of light is an active process, requiring the direct involvement of the individual seeking enlightenment. We must understand that all elements of life are suitable targets for the work of enlightenment; only as we individualize the light does it radiate through our own life.

We do not need to become a missionary in Africa to find light—or retire to a monastery or ashram and ape the movements of saints. Our work, hobbies, relationships, responsibilities, and efforts to grow are the suitable and proper vehicles for light. They provide us rich opportunity for discovering the light, comprehending it, integrating it, and expressing it. Unless we focus the light through these activities, whatever they may be, we will not really be doing its work.

There is no moment too insignificant to use this formula. After all, if we cannot be an agent of light in the midst of annoyance or pettiness or simple fatigue, it is hardly reasonable to expect to be an agent of light in more spectacular circumstances. If we cannot be faithful in a little, it is foolish to believe we could be faithful over much. If we cannot heal, build, and serve with light, even in the smallest of ways, we cannot rightly expect to be healed, strengthened, or served by the light ourself. Therefore, to receive light, we must learn to contribute light. To be enlightened, we must become an agent of light.

Which prepares us for becoming the light itself.

1.

An Introduction to Spiritual Integration

One of the great hardships confronting the agent of light is the deprivation which accompanies the need to work in relative isolation from the source of light he seeks to represent and serve. In order for the invisible to become visible and the abstract to become tangible, the wholeness of life must be fragmented into separate parts. The beauty of light cannot flower on earth except through the individual creations of nature and mankind. The benevolent power of light cannot walk on earth except through the compassionate acts of individual humans. Spirit must be given form, so it can specialize and interact with the rest of creation. But the risk of specialization is separation from the light of God. In this risk lie the seeds of all misery and confusion.

Of course, spirit never actually loses its wholeness, even when it invests itself in specialization. It remains integrated with its creative purpose and identity, a part of the larger whole. The problem of isolation arises primarily for the human personality. We often become so immersed in our chores and duties on the physical plane that we forget we are an agent of light. We forget we are part of a larger whole, and become absorbed in "making it on our own"—because we believe we will receive no help from anyone else. As a result, we become estranged from the light within us, from true companionship with others, and from the wholeness of life. The world in which we think and act and move becomes darkened and confined, cut off from its true source like a flower snipped from a plant by a thoughtless child.

Yet the need to work in isolation from the source of light, amid the shadows and restrictions of earth, does not in any way exclude us from a real and continuous identification with light. The light of God is constantly reaching out to embrace us—if we will but respond and embrace it. Indeed, there is a special relationship between the individual and the whole—a relationship which allows us to contribute to the progress of the whole while drawing from it the support we need to act. As the poet Alexander Pope put it in his masterpiece, *An Essay on Man*:

God loves from Whole to Parts: But human soul
Must rise from Individual to Whole.
Self-love but serves the virtuous mind to wake,

As the small pebble stirs the peaceful lake;
The centre moved, a circle straight succeeds,
Another still, and still another spreads;
Friend, parent, neighbour, first it will embrace;
His country next; and next all human race;
Wide and more wide, th' o'erflowings of the mind
Take every creature in, of every kind;
Earth smiles around, with boundless bounty blest,
And Heaven beholds its image in his breast.

To be an effective agent of light, we must recognize this special relationship and learn to "rise from Individual to Whole." We need to see the larger contexts of life in which we live and move and have our being and embrace them, integrating them into our life in meaningful ways. Simply put, our personal attitudes must not be isolated from our common sense and wisdom. Our fears and doubts need not be divorced from our capacity for courage. We are designed for wholeness, even though we specialize the light within us as an individual. We are meant to express heaven in our life, even though we sometimes fumble in error and falter in our progress.

Yet this sense of wholeness is not bestowed upon us automatically. There is only one way to achieve it: by learning the techniques of spiritual integration.

Genuine integration does more than merely touch the light; it embraces it. It links the wholeness of light with our individual capacities to focus the light, thereby creating an important bridge in consciousness. Through this bridge, the power of light can be infused into our habits, practices, behavior, ideas, and responsibilities, transforming them into expressions of a much higher quality than before.

In a very real way, spiritual integration is a magical process. Whether it is used to link abstract ideas with concrete applications, join the light of spirit to the aspirations of the personality, coordinate our emotions with our thoughts, or harmonize our efforts with those of others, the goal of integration always is to produce a final whole which is greater than the sum total of the parts—a more powerful idea, a better person, a more enlightened self-expression, or more effective cooperation. As such, integration is something far more important than the simple act of assembling disparate units or "putting things together," just as a finished oil painting is far more than a mere collection of colors. For in addition to paint, the artist has applied inspiration, skill, joy, wisdom, and a sense of beauty to his canvas—and in the process has integrated the colors on his palette and the ideas in his head to produce a new creation.

It is this magic of integration which enables us to translate the context of God's wholeness into skills and talents which serve our individual self-expression. But we are the magician, the one who must pull the rabbit of integration out of the hat of our needs and requirements. The words of a great orator are no more powerful than the sounds of a grunting hog, except that he has assembled them into a dynamic unity and sent them marching forth as a masterful articulation of grand ideas. The spools of thread of a master weaver are no more creative than the balls of yarn a cat might tangle up, except that the weaver has the capacity to transform his threads into majestic tapestries. A group of doctors and nurses is really nothing but a crowd of people, except when they merge their skills and ability to cooperate as a team of professionals performing delicate surgery. Just so, a human being is but a shadow of what he can become, until he learns to coordinate his thoughts, feelings, and acts and integrate them with the love and guidance of light.

And yet, the magic of integration is not widely recognized. Much has been written about integration, extolling its virtues as a psychological practice, but most of these writings have failed to understand its true scope. They have failed to embrace the light.

Many people assume, for example, that personal integration involves gathering together the ingredients of ambition, faith, nerve, and skill, and working toward success. But once they have assembled these elements, they often still do not know what to do with them. They have great faith, but their faith is undermined by pockets of doubt and fear. They have great skill, but their efforts are sabotaged by discouragement and despair. They have great courage and ambition but express them without tact and goodwill, thereby embarrassing themselves. Such people have not yet discovered the magic of integration, which uses faith to eliminate doubt and fear, skill to dominate discouragement, and goodwill and gracefulness to modify boorishness and greed.

Others try to approach integration by substituting force

for magic. Instead of recognizing the power of light to embrace and transform that which is not yet whole, these people try to impose a state of integration by decree. To the degree they can enforce their desire with arrogance and intimidation, they usually obtain what they want. But it is never true integration—just an uneasy state of truce and capitulation. The forces of dissent and rebellion rage and seethe in unseen realms, damaging both victim and victor, even though conditions may appear peaceful superficially. A common example of this kind of "integration" can be found in families dominated by petty dictators, who insist that everyone else bow to their demands, in the name of "family unity." It can also be found in the way some people approach the integration of their own unruly habits and urges.

Sometimes, integration is confused for compromise. A person who has made a serious mistake, for example, may attempt to compensate for it by feeling guilty about it. The guilt helps him feel better about the mistake, but does absolutely nothing to correct it. There are many variations on this particular theme, most of them involving some kind of moral equivocation or rationalization. An individual who habitually cheats in certain circumstances may be scrupulously honest in others, so he can pretend to be a person of integrity. A fellow who is uncaring to most people may be quite tender and affectionate to a few, so he can believe himself a loving individual. Needless to say, nothing is being integrated in these instances except fantasies and flaws. Genuine integration, by contrast, embraces the ideals of life and focuses them on our imperfections, so they can be healed and rendered more perfect. Just as soapy water integrated with dirty hands leads to clean fingers, so also the integration of joy, goodwill, and courage with sadness, resentment, and fear leads to a purified and healthy state free of these negativities.

The most common misunderstanding of integration, however, is the belief that we can integrate consciousness simply by blending or mixing the diverse elements within it. There is much talk in our modern age, for example, of the integration of mind and body. But the vast majority of people who claim to profess an interest in this work seem to end up using the mind primarily to rationalize continued indulgences in physical cravings and vanity! Instead of working toward the ideal of using the physical form to produce creative expressions of brilliant ideas—which would be true integration—these people seem to find it easier simply to use the mind to gloat over their physical prowess and beauty.

A similar tendency can be observed in most efforts to integrate the mind with the emotions. It more frequently produces a set of intellectual rationalizations which protect our selfishness and desires than a genuine transformation of feeling and greater maturity. There is the appearance that worthwhile changes have occurred, but they all represent a step backward in growth, not forward.

In our efforts to "rise from Individual to Whole," we must be careful not to dilute the magic of integration in these ways, but work instead toward its real goals.

Whether we are striving to integrate our personality with our soul, or to coordinate our personal efforts with those of others, we should always start by defining the larger context which will be our guiding ideal—the center of "the peaceful lake" which, once stirred, propels circles of movement to the outer boundary of the lake, embracing it in its entirety. It is the effort to cultivate a relationship with this central principle or ideal, and infuse it into our life, which generates the magic of spiritual integration and distinguishes it from lesser practices.

The actual work of integration occurs in four steps:

1. Through alignment. This could be an alignment of our emotions with a spiritual ideal, or alignment of our enthusiasm with the work of a group, or alignment of our activities with our skills, time, and opportunities. Alignment with an ideal is something more than just an awareness of it, however; it is the work of adopting a proper posture toward it. When integrating a higher element with a lower one, for example, proper alignment results in the lower serving and responding to the higher, not the reverse.

2. Through interaction. We do not merely bask meditatively in the light of the soul but interact with it, harnessing its wisdom and love to penetrate to the roots of our confusion and selfishness and overcome them. As a citizen of a nation, we do not just take its benefits of citizenship for granted, but work for the common good and honor our responsibilities.

3. Through transformation. Where there is conflict and opposition, integration draws the warring factions

together, sets them in a new and more enlightened context of wholeness, and heals the rift. Where there is chaos and disunity, integration draws the unconnected elements together and instills a common sense of purpose, producing fusion. Where there is immaturity, integration draws in new elements of wisdom, producing growth.

4. Through the emergence of a new identity. Having embraced a new measure of light, we are something more than we were before. We are better able to act and serve. Whenever integration truly occurs, then "Earth smiles around, with boundless bounty blest—and Heaven beholds its image in our breast."

There are three rich areas which afford us opportunities for putting the magic of integration to work for our personal benefit and gain: the inner dimensions of our consciousness, the responsibilities and opportunities of our daily life, and time.

In working to integrate the inner dimensions of consciousness, our goal should always be to increase our responsiveness to the highest and most noble elements within ourself. In other words, we should strive to embrace the light and become a better agent of it. Ignorance should be integrated with wisdom, leaving only brilliance and creativity. Self-centeredness should be integrated with brotherhood, leaving only the capacity to care and serve. Fear should be integrated with courage, leaving us ready to act with integrity. Laziness should be integrated with the motivating power of light, leaving us willing to initiate activity. In these ways, we integrate our:

- Conduct with our intentions.
- Emotions with our mind.
- Ideas with our ideals.
- Body with its purpose.
- Personality with the light of spirit.

The effort to integrate with our responsibilities and the opportunities of daily life proceeds in much the same way, but with the primary goal of embracing the light we find outside ourself, instead of within. We find that the "special relationship" of the individual to the whole can apply to our interaction with friends, loved ones, work, religious worship, citizenship, and the other activities of daily life just as meaningfully as it does to our interaction with spirit. But to establish it, we must integrate with the light of these outer activities. We must see the work we do as an enlightened contribution to humanity, not an insult or inconvenience. We must view our relationships with friends as a mutual expression of light, rather than a source of self-gratification. We must view problems as opportunities to grow, not threats to our well-being. In these ways, we integrate our:

- Work with our destiny.
- Roles in life with our spiritual values.
- Relationships with our capacity for goodwill.
- Religious worship with the work of spirit.
- Duties as citizens with the spirit of the nation.

The third great area for integration is with time. To most people, time is just an antagonist, a force they are always at odds with. They have failed to see the larger context of time and realize that time is a creation of light. To integrate with time, we must become aware of the patterns of history, the cycles of right timing, and the opportunities which even the shortest span of time afford us—and learn to relate the past with the present and our potential for the future. In these ways, we integrate our:

- Personal efforts with the cycles of the zodiac.
- Problems of the past with our current potential.
- Fears of the future with the promise of success.
- Capacity to act with the ideal of right timing.

A simple exercise which can help us learn the lessons of embracing the light is to choose a major aspect of life and identify the values and ideals we are expressing—or ought to be expressing—through it. The area chosen could be something from the inner dimensions of life, such as our emotions, self-image, or ethics; it could be an outer activity, such as the way we interact with others; or it could be our perspective on time.

In defining the value or ideal this is meant to serve, we should strive to tap the very center of this particular part of our life, and embrace its light. This includes assessing what is right in this part of our life—and what it ideally can become.

It does not include, however, a morbid evaluation of what is wrong or an excessive identification with hurt feelings. These elements may well be more apparent to us than the ideal, but they do not lead us to the center from which we must act.

In other words, we must think about this aspect of

our life and not just react emotionally to it, as so many people do. We must discover the larger context in which this part of our life makes sense. Once this preliminary evaluation has been made, we can then pursue the four steps of integration:

• We align our personal values with the ideals of the larger context. Do we need to revise our values? How can we act more effectively in honoring the greater whole?

• We interact with the force and wisdom of these values and ideals. How can we translate them into daily behavior and practical ideas? How will we benefit by doing so?

• We transform our current attitudes and conduct, by mentally rehearsing specific ways of expressing these ideals and values in the circumstances of daily living.

• We achieve a new identity, by seeing ourself as something greater than we were before. Having enriched our thoughts and feelings with a new measure of light, we should never again think of ourself in the limited ways of the past. We are now more truly than ever an agent of light, able to embrace the light of the world.

And be embraced by it.

2.

Obstacles to Integration

Integration is the effort to incorporate the transcendent, abstract elements of life into our own daily self-expression—to bring heaven to earth. The process of integration relies on a deep, intense aspiration for the highest and the best, but it involves a great deal more than aspiration alone. It requires an act of spiritual engineering: we must build a bridge in consciousness between earth and heaven—between the personality and spirit—and then import something of heaven into our acts and beliefs and values. As Alexander Pope put it: "We must rise from Individual to Whole."

This engineering project involves two challenges: to build the bridge across the apparent gap between us and God, and then to traverse it with regularity, until we have enriched the many facets of our life with divine love, wisdom, and joy.

Unfortunately, these two requirements are often overlooked by earnest but naïve seekers. The bridge that would link us to the transcendent levels does not exist, and it will not exist until we build it! We cannot wait for funding from the federal highways program, nor hitch a ride with a fellow aspirant. The potential and design for the bridge exist, of course, as part of the archetypal structure of the divine mind. But the bridge itself must be built by each agent of light on his or her own.

In the last chapter, we outlined four steps in the work of integration: alignment, interaction, transformation, and the emergence of a new identity. Yet it is possible to follow these steps with reasonable diligence and still not achieve integration. Just because blueprints exist does not mean that the bridge builder will follow them!

There are therefore two highly important questions each of us must ask ourself:

How complete is our bridge? What additional work must be done in order to construct an unimpeded line of contact with spirit? What is missing from our bridge? Is our bridge too weak?

What obstacles have we strewn upon the bridge? What prevents us from traversing it? Do we charge ourself a heavy toll of guilt or fear just to set foot on the bridge? What garbage and debris is piling up in the middle of the span, making it impossible to get to the other side?

The elements which may be missing from our bridge

to heaven might include a lack of commitment, but there are a number of other important candidates as well:

· Difficulty in working with abstract thought. Even if we have a brilliant intellect, we may find it hard to transcend our doubts and sense of boundary and begin working directly and fully with divine principles and archetypal forces. As a result, we are unable to embrace the larger picture Pope was describing in the phrase "from Individual to Whole."

· A tepid measure of faith. Each time we manage to cross the bridge and bring something of spirit back with us, we need to strengthen our faith that spirit is our ultimate source of all good things and our most potent resource for healing and growth. Faith is the substance of the pillars that support our bridge; it sustains us in moments of doubt and despair.

· A lack of self-discipline. Bridge-building takes effort. We must strive to grow as an agent of light every day. Haphazard efforts lead to rickety, unsafe bridges. Only regular, repetitive use of correct techniques can build a proper connection with the best within us.

Even if our bridge is solid and sturdy, however, we may still have allowed debris and waste to accumulate, thereby blocking the flow of traffic in both directions. Examples of this debris might include:

Fear. Great measures of enthusiasm and devotion can be dashed in a moment by a single wave of fear—especially fear of what we may learn about ourself if we continue to push on across the bridge.

Pessimism. Optimism opens our mind so that it is

capable of identifying with the vastness of our inner potential and design. Pessimism shrinks the scope of our mind and emphasizes the seeming hopelessness of our situation.

Guilt. Because we do not understand why we are here, we often convince ourself that we are not worthy of associating with spirit. It is natural to make mistakes; we should learn from them and proceed. It is unhealthy to wallow morbidly in a sense of guilt or failure.

Self-doubt. The personality tends to doubt that even its best efforts will be enough. The soul knows better; it works from design and certainty. Where we have let self-doubt accumulate, however, it cuts off the soul's vision of success.

As we investigate these conditions, we are apt to find that most of the design flaws in the bridge and the debris that has piled up are of our own making. It is therefore our responsibility to make repairs and prove that we are ready to succeed.

The first place to inspect for obstacles is in the nature of our alignment. The work of alignment in integration occurs as we focus our attention more and more on the qualities of spirit. As we make decisions, we try to view issues from the larger perspective of the higher self. As we deal with people, we strive to interact with the best within them.

In this regard, the most serious problem may be that we are building our bridge—our connection to spirit—to something other than spirit. Many people, for example, plug themselves into their subconscious fantasies—in the name of spirit! Such people end up praying to their own deep fears and desires for guidance, healing, and instruction. Instead of crossing a bridge, they are just walking a plank—into the depths of their fantasies.

The tendency of the average Christian to pray to an image of a sweet, gentle, sad, and wimpy Jesus—forever forgiving of everything, and expecting nothing from us—is a good example of a bridge to nowhere in particular. This popular image misses the true nature of the Christ by a galaxy or two.

Other aspirants align themselves to the group mind of a cult, or even a denomination. Again, they fall far short of contacting spirit. They contact only the collective dogma and delusions of the group.

Perhaps the most common error of alignment occurs when aspirants align themselves with diluted concepts or feelings of love, forgiveness, devotion, or joy, rather than the true spiritual force. Aligning ourself with a desire to be pampered and excused from all unpleasantness is merely selfishness masquerading as compassion. It does not lead to integration—it can only lead to delusion and mischief.

The self-made debris and garbage that interferes with the work of alignment tend to be generated by a nonchalant attitude toward the need for personal growth and change. Some people assume, for instance, that God will do all the work of growth on their behalf. They claim to be "born again," but they keep on approaching life with the same arrogance and stupidity as before. The central work of integration is the growth and transformation of the personality. If we try to avoid growing, or believe that we know enough already, or think that our problems are caused by the faults of others and society, then we will have genuine trouble making any meaningful kind of alignment with spirit. We are too busy making excuses, playing the victim, and waiting for divine magic or miracles to rescue us.

Some people keep a radio playing without ever listening to it; the music or talk is just so much noise in the background. They never actually interact with it, either mentally or emotionally; it has no meaning in their lives.

For many people, the life of spirit is very much like the radio. Even though they are aware of it, they never actually listen to it—or try to respond to its guidance. In fact, it is possible to have built the bridge of integration, through faith, prayer, and self-discipline, yet seldom use it to interact with the spiritual forces to be found on the other end.

For integration to succeed, we must cross the bridge that links us to spirit and actively acquire new measures of spiritual wisdom, love, and power—which we then express in appropriate ways in our daily life. Just as it would be silly to go to a grocery store, buy food, and then leave it in the grocery cart when we get in our car and drive home, it is foolish to visit the life of spirit but come back empty-handed.

There are many obstacles which prevent us from

interacting effectively with spirit.   One of the most common lies in trust. Many people who believe in God nonetheless do not trust in divine life to protect them, guide them, or nurture them.   Even though they view the life of spirit as desirable, they regard it as something separate from their life. They place God "up there," unavailable to them while they struggle "down here."

And yet, none of these people has any trouble interacting with fear, gloom, or pessimism. They have built their bridges, but they are bridges to the dark side of living. They need to dismantle these links, and replace them with a strong connection to the life of spirit. In specific, they need to discover and learn to cherish the value and power of spiritual forces—spiritual forces such as peace, harmony, goodwill, and wisdom.

The great difficulty in dismantling the false bridges to darkness is that they have become part of the fabric of life. Every expression of fear strengthens their link to fear. Every moment of anger is a bridge to greater indignation. Every sensation of guilt magnifies a sense of wrong-doing.

It is a cycle which will never end—until they decide to stop it.

How do we eventually halt and reverse these cycles? Through the third stage of integration—transformation. We come to recognize how destructive our anger, fear, and guilt have been, and learn that the only way to eliminate these poisons is to purge them with spirit. Where there has been anger, we must cultivate helpfulness. Where there has been fear, we must develop a sense of love. Where there has been guilt, we must nurture an expression of nobility and worth.

We do this work slowly, deliberately, by cultivating the practical expression of each of these spiritual energies—helpfulness, love, and nobility. We saturate ourself with the light of spirit, burning away the patterns of anger, fear, and shame that have held us captive for so long. Eventually, the anger, fear, and shame are scrubbed out of our awareness entirely, leaving only a newborn potential for spiritual expression.

But even the work of transformation can be sabotaged by hidden obstacles. One of the most common is compartmentalization. Many people prolong their agony by exempting protected aspects of their life from spiritual scrutiny. As long as they treat their friends with goodwill, for instance, they figure that it is acceptable to treat their enemies with contempt and hostility. Or, as long as they are honest in public dealings, they can cheat in privacy. In this way, they split their consciousness in twain. One part will be integrated with spirit, while the other will be integrated with low passions.

Another great obstacle is the acceptance of lowered standards. Anger is all right, many people insist, so long as it is righteous, or directed only at truly nasty people. Deep despair is similarly acceptable, so long as it is the result of a genuine loss. Doubt is also all right—so long as it is our doubt!

None of these common beliefs is true, of course, but

many of us like to pretend otherwise. As a result, we build our bridge to self-deception, not spirit.

One of the most amazing obstacles to integration is the common religious belief in the west that actual growth is not necessary. We are saved, some of us believe, just because we have accepted the right dogma. Because we have been reborn, nothing else is required—not even transformation. We can be as lazy and as irresponsible as we want. After all, we believe.

Sadly, this kind of belief is a bridge only to fantasy. It has no spiritual validity.

The presumptions of the personality can also be enormous hindrances. Many good people conclude, sometime in their lives, that they have suffered enough, and so they quit striving. These people are "kicking against the pricks," as Paul described it—they are rebelling against the very factors of life that are trying to help them grow out of their confusion and immaturity. They believe themselves to be willing to grow, but have reached a point where they think that life is demanding too much of them. So they "draw the line" and expect God to observe it. "God will have to love me just the way I am," they decide.

At this point, transformation is next to impossible.

The final stage of integration is the emergence of a new identity—the true process of being born anew. We begin to perceive a greater presence of spirit in our life, in terms of a new willingness to forgive, a deeper appreciation of life, and expanded creativity. We begin to view our work and family from a higher, more inclusive perspective. We find that we are more comfortable with unpleasant memories from the past and with enemies; we have exchanged hostility for helpfulness, and fear for courage. We likewise become aware of the greater possibilities of our life and work.

The primary obstacle we must contend with at this stage of integration is incompleteness. We fail to follow through on work that we begin. We apologize for harm that we have done without compensating for it. Or we recognize mistakes we have made without changing our character to make sure we never repeat them.

The great example of incompleteness in our modern life is the popular notion that it is okay to be a selfish, immature person so long as we have accepted responsibility for it. These people never change; they just cover up the messes they make and move on. This is not transformation! Nor does it succeed in integrating any measure of spirit into our consciousness.

We can eliminate much of the struggle of integration by learning to recognize and triumph over these obstacles as they arise. There is a simple exercise which will help us detect and defeat these problems.

The exercise begins by recognizing an area of great emptiness in our life. This sense of emptiness exists because we have not filled it with some facet of spirit. Perhaps we are joyless. Or passive. Or untrusting. In each case, there is one common element that is missing in our life–spirit.

We should evaluate this emptiness in terms of the four aspects of integration.

What spiritual quality must we align with in order to eliminate this emptiness? How can we align with it? What attitudes, assumptions, and beliefs are blocking this alignment? How can we remove these blocks and align with true spiritual forces?

What are we interacting with which keeps us from paying attention to spirit? How can we stop interacting with this negativity and begin interacting with spirit? As an example, if we resent other people for the limits they have placed on our life, how can we begin to eliminate this resentment? What must we do to gain a larger perspective on the value of these people in our life?

Then, we should consider the steps to be taken to link our emptiness with the richness of spirit. In what ways must we grow in order to better express the power of spirit? How can we change in our own approach to living? What must we learn about drawing our fears into the light of love, or drawing our arrogance into the light of humility and piety? This is not an intellectual exercise; we must learn to use spiritual force to transform our own habits, attitudes, and traits.

Finally, we must begin thinking of ourself as a spiritually-enriched person, not the same old empty shell we have been for so long. We must carry with us the presence of joy or wisdom or trust or humility, so that we can rely on it and use it as life presents us with new challenges—and new obstacles.

If we do, we will quickly learn a powerful truth—that

within each of us lies the power to build a strong and stable bridge to spirit—a bridge that we can traverse in order to bring into our life new measures of divine life. The process of building this bridge, integration, begins as we decide to clear away the obstacles in our life that might impede this work.

3.

The Basis
for Integration

The heart of the great illusion is our sense of *separative-ness*—our belief that we human beings are "down here," stumbling our way through life on earth, while God, if there is one, is somewhere "up there," sitting on his or her throne in heaven, barely aware of our suffering and hardships. We further complicate this illusion by believing that the gap which creates this separation is a punishment imposed upon us. We reinforce these beliefs with doctrines such as original sin, and extend the state of separativeness to the whole human race as well. We each seem to struggle in divinely-sanctioned isolation.

When we examine the record of divisiveness and conflict in the human family, it is easy to believe that these theories have merit. Humanity seems to thrive on its adversarial nature, pitting one group against another. Our history is the story of "us versus them." It seems as though the only time we all come together is to plead the case of "us versus God"—an uncaring, unsympathetic God who divorced himself from humanity eons ago. Many people, for example, believe that in every situation, someone must win and everyone else must lose. To them, the possibility that everyone could win is nonexistent. And they can be very persuasive in stating their case.

This notion of alienation and separation is very popular today; it saturates every seam in modern philosophy and government. It is the message of existentialism—and the credo of communism. But it is false. It only describes what seems to be—the grand illusion—not what actually is.

The truth is stated by Paul in the Bible: "We are all members of the same body, the body of Christ." In other words, we live and move and have our being in the One Life of God. Nor is this just a Christian belief; it is a statement of reality confirmed by every major religion. We are not separate, either from God or from one another. We are united in the One Life of spirit.

The reality of Oneness is symbolized even during physical life. Our physical bodies are made from a common pool of physical substance that the Bible refers to as "dust." While animated by spirit, these bodies seem to be individualistic. But when the body dies, it returns to dust and becomes part of the common pool again.

Not everyone sees the meaning of this symbolism, however, and these people are faced with a paradox. If we are united in Oneness at the level of spirit, they wonder, why are we not One at the physical level? Can we achieve Oneness while alive on earth? And if we can, how do we do it?

The answer is simple. The part does not always recognize the Whole. It is often immersed in ignorance. But the reality of the Whole never changes. Even while the part ignorantly denies any connection to the Whole, the Whole nonetheless embraces the sum of all the parts. It also knows the purpose and design of these parts, and supports them, individually and collectively, so that they can live up to this purpose and design.

If we have been hiking for ten miles, after all, our feet are apt to be tired. If they could decide what to do, they would vote to quit. But we may know that we are only a mile or two from our destination, where a good meal and a warm bed awaits us. So we override the preferences of the feet, which do not understand—but are happy with our decision once we reach our goal!

In the same way, we often do not understand the soul's purpose or plan—or God's purpose or plan, for that matter. But God knows. And so does the soul. If we keep tramping along, we, too, will know—once we reach our goal.

The relationship of the part to the Whole is the basis for the work of spiritual integration. It lets the individual recognize and become an active, conscious part of the larger body or system of which it is a part—the greater spiritual scheme of things—even when we do not fully understand them.

Divine life promotes integration and wholeness as an

automatic process of life. At the deepest core of being, life is one, whole, and complete. And all of creation is designed to fulfill and embody this wholeness.

In other words, because we have been created in the image of God, there exists within each of us a strong impulse to rediscover our spiritual wholeness—our connections with divine life. This deep-seated impulse consists of four elements:

- Purpose, derived from divine will.
- Plan, derived from Hierarchical focus.
- Inclusive love, derived from our Christ nature.
- Law, derived from divine intelligence.

These four elements are at work within us, helping us move toward better integration. They function as designed, whether we believe in them or not, or accept them or not—just as our lungs continue to breathe whether or not we know about oxygen. If we cooperate with them, we can see the results of their activity in the growth we make—growth in maturity, in wisdom, in goodwill, and in talent. If we do not cooperate with them, we can still see the results of their activity—but the evidence will be framed in the context of loss, sorrow, suffering, and perhaps even defeat, instead of growth. This is not because God punishes us for our resistance, but because our resistance alienates us from the opportunities, healing, blessings, and talent that spirit is trying to guide us toward.

All of creation responds to the basic keynote of integration. In fact, it can truthfully be stated that integration is a basic fact of life—a fundamental property, like gravity.

If we can understand the process of integration, then we can harness it for our own use. In so doing, we will tap into enormous spiritual power to work effectively in our life. But as long as we remain ignorant of this process and its value to us, we will probably continue to perpetuate an adversarial posture—toward ourselves, toward life, toward our friends and colleagues, toward the soul, and toward God.

The human soul is a microcosm of divine life. As such, it fully embodies all four basic elements of integration:

• It sets its goals and evaluates its accomplishments based on a fundamental awareness of purpose. It is impelled by divine will.

• It creates a detailed, thorough plan of evolution for itself and its successive personalities based on the greater design of all humanity.

• It acts always under the motivation of all-inclusive love. It is never adversarial. It strives to work always as a perfect part of a perfect Whole.

• It seeks always to fulfill the promise of divine law. It is not interested in short cuts or quick fixes. It strives to reproduce the glory of God in all that it does.

Part of the assignment of any soul is the creation and supervision of personalities that appear for a period of time on earth and then withdraw. Although many people on earth remain ignorant of the fact, the soul is heavily involved in planning, supporting, and guiding the life and accomplishments of each personality. Indeed, its presence and support is constant and profound.

Even though its motives for growing and acting are often very much at odds with the motives of the personality, the soul continues to help each personality define and fulfill its own commitment to purpose, plan, love, and law. Even in immature personalities, the soul has an enormous impact. Long before the personality is born, the soul defines the type of temperament it wants the personality to have, based on past experiences, current cycles of human evolution, the needs of the personality's "group," and much more. It selects family members, interests, talents, and lessons to be mastered.

In one life, the soul may choose to limit the personality with a handicap, in the expectation that the personality will surmount it. In another, it may construct a mind that is capable of registering subtlety and divine wisdom. It may strengthen our sense of discovery and innovativeness—or, it may mute these attributes, so that we will remain practical and not be swept away by fantasy. It can amplify our sense of right and wrong—our ethic—or it may leave us vulnerable, to be tested by the events of life. Finally, it may bless us with large quantities of hope, vision, and faith, as well as an undying commitment to growth—or it may heighten our resistance, so that we can learn how we put limits on ourself.

Most people, of course, never become aware that these decisions have already been made for them—or that they were made by their own higher intelligence, the soul. But the seeds of all of this "planning" do ex-

46

ist and influence us, even if they only exist at hidden, unconscious levels.

An intelligent personality will seek out and try to understand these seeds. By making contact with them, we can greatly expand our connection with higher intelligence—and we can integrate more fully with these patterns and plans. Nonetheless, all too many personalities do not respond in this enlightened way. They ignore or even reject the guidance and love of the soul. They rebel against it—often while proclaiming their love and devotion to it! They are willing to love the soul—if it will just stay up in heaven with God and behave like a loyal servant catering to the whims of the personality! But if the soul persists in trying to guide and direct the life of the personality, they will not be interested in cooperating.

Fortunately, this rebellion is only a temporary condition—although a painful one for as long as we persist in it. Ultimately, the soul becomes more and more skilled in its ability to impose its plan and purpose on the personality—even a wayward one. It does not use coercion to accomplish this; rather, it patiently and tirelessly draws the personality into its loving, nurturing sphere of influence. As the personality grows in skill and insight, this invitation of the soul becomes more and more irresistible.

The rebellious personality is like a camper who insists on starting a fire with wet wood. Eventually, he learns that it makes more sense to cooperate with the laws of combustion, rather than fight them!

The sooner we begin cooperating with the inner design of the soul for its personality—and the divine laws that it serves—the easier and more fulfilling our life will become. Understanding this, the agent of light tries to embrace the innovative reforms of integration, not fight them. He learns the value of integrating new light into the human mind, and new love into the human heart. His priorities begin to change. Instead of being self-absorbed, he becomes interested in reuniting with the soul. Instead of being separative and defensive, he becomes interested in integrating with divine life.

This sets the stage for spiritual transformation.

The work of integration requires more than just the realization that the soul already possesses the basic elements of integration: purpose, plan, love, and law. The personality must build up a strong base of compatible attributes. Otherwise, there will be nothing of substance that can respond to the transforming work of the love or intelligence of the soul.

This is the reason why every step of growth involves more than just removing some inhibition that "blocks" the personality. We must also replace the block with a spiritually-inspired quality or skill.

Not all human talents fit this requirement. A capacity to hit a baseball five hundred feet is not something the soul can use as a basis for integration. But a deep respect for one's competitors and teammates might well be a character trait that can be successfully used.

In fact, most of the capacities and traits that will let a

personality integrate with the soul are common and ordinary aspects of human living—for example, the nurturing love with which a parent raises his or her children. While it is true that some parents use their children selfishly, it is equally true that some make great sacrifices in order to help their children grow up wise, happy, and healthy. These are the kinds of skills and abilities that could then become the basis for integrative work.

The most common of these human capacities include:

1. Our sense of identity. The moment we start asking: "Who am I?" we set the stage for discovering that we are the creation of a higher self, the soul. The more we can identify with this higher self and its needs, the more fully we become integrated. As we also learn to respond wisely and fully to the direction of the soul, our ability to integrate spiritual forces into our character and talent expands.

2. Our values and beliefs. Our world view is one of the greatest raw materials the soul can use in promoting integration. If we view the world selfishly, thinking always of what others can do to help us, there will be little room for meaningful growth. But if we are always looking for new ways to help others and society, even when it is personally inconvenient, then there exists a solid foundation for the work of integration.

3. Our priorities. It is possible to have noble values and principles, yet pay little attention to them. In order for integration to proceed, we must adopt a set of personal objectives similar to those of the soul.

4. Our intentions. Some people adopt noble values

and objectives, but without any true intention to activate them in their lives. These people profess to be peacemakers, for instance, yet continue to act in divisive, selfish ways. Unless our intentions are aligned with spiritual design, not much integration will occur.

5. Our awareness. One of the key elements in any work of spiritual integration is the measure of awareness we direct toward the soul. Do we remember how the soul has helped us in the past? Do we recall times in the past when the soul has shown us the solutions to problems? One of the basic laws of life is that energy follows attention. If we focus on how the soul has already helped us integrate, we can make the process much easier.

It must be understood that these basic capacities must be responsive to spirit before any spiritual integration can occur. If our sense of identity is devoted to being a victim, and we try to integrate our personality on this basis, the attempt will be a disaster. We will weaken our personal strength, rather than enrich it. If we embrace greed as a high and noble value, we will eclipse the guidance and intent of the soul.

It is therefore always important to keep spirit at the heart of all work of integration. Unless the power to integrate emanates from spirit, the process may go awry and produce a Frankenstein monster.

A good place to begin the work of integration, therefore, is to survey our personality and see what talents and capacities that we already possess can be used as a basis for integration. This inventory can be conducted by asking ourself:

Who are we? How do we define ourself? In terms of accomplishments and who we know? In terms of our status in society or the size of our income? Or do we recognize ourself as a child of God, a spark of pure light?

What are our primary values and beliefs? How do we view the world? Are we optimistic? Do we think that we can become a better person? Is there meaning in life? How do we respond to challenges? As opportunities—or as insults?

What are our priorities? When conflicting demands arise—comfort, duty, sacrifice, service, or avoidance—what do we put first? Do we try to control others? Are we primarily interested in getting attention? Are we able to work without recognition?

What motivates us? Are we primarily focused in avoiding suffering and seeking comfort? Or do we recognize an inner urge to seek out higher opportunities and achievements that lead us to new divine possibilities?

On what do we focus our awareness? Are we caught up in fads, styles, prejudices, and flash? Or have we learned to think for ourself? Are we striving to discover the larger ramifications of life—and solve the mysteries of spirit?

As we investigate each category, it is then important to evaluate our responses. How can we make these characteristics or attributes more responsive to the design of our soul?

4.

The Tools of Integration

The essence of integration is inclusiveness—the divine principle of love. We become aware of an ideal, a law, a purpose, or a divine force which is not a part of our character, then expand our character to embrace it and, as we gain skill, to express it on a daily basis. We include within our personal system something that previously was not a part of it.

The work of inclusiveness occurs in many simple ways. Our well-trained mind may become aware of an inconsistency or double standard within our character—or perhaps just a need for better coordination of our thinking and feeling. In response to this need, it defines what is lacking—what element of spirit is missing from our character that would resolve the double standard or provide better coordination. The mind then draws in this missing element and seeks to embody it in its daily thinking and acting, thereby producing greater wholeness.

This capacity for inclusiveness is a talent any intelligent individual can develop. The need for such skill is not widely recognized, however—nor widely taught.

Because most adults do not have any working familiarity with the power of inclusiveness, most of them suffer from some kind of dys-integration. By default, they have allowed huge gaps to develop and widen in their personal psychology. In most cases, they have also allowed the basic illusion of separativeness to estrange them from their own higher consciousness—the light of spirit.

These inconsistences may be quite ordinary. A person might be highly organized and efficient at work, but disorganized and chaotic at home. Others may be gracious hosts and hostesses with friends, but crabby and suspicious when dealing with strangers. Another might be tolerant about religion but narrowminded and biased about politics. Some may be at peace with the present, but haunted by the past. The possible variations are endless.

Obviously, it is not very intelligent to try to live with these internal handicaps. An intelligent person should want to be able to face every day with:

• A profound sense of consistency, knowing that his acts and deeds will be a true expression of his character, which in turn is seamlessly linked with the higher realms of spirit.

• An active measure of harmony, based on a deep sense of inner serenity and the proven knowledge that we are in tune with our highest ideals and plans.

• The power to contribute something significant to life, rather than having to spend most of our time sorting out the messes we have already created.

• A sense of control—a basic awareness that the authority of spirit can flow unimpeded through our character into self-expression. We do not have to fight worries, fears, paranoias, and other negative forces that will demand that we pay more attention to them than to our chosen work.

• A clear conscience, based on the knowledge that we have always tried to serve the best within us. As we make mistakes, as everyone does, we correct them as soon as possible, then proceed with our activity with a clean slate.

While none of these states of mind comes automatically, it is equally true that no one ever needs to suffer the devastating consequences of dys-integration. Integration is an option every intelligent human can choose. It is a choice between inclusiveness and estrangement, self-mastery and victimhood.

The sane choices are inclusiveness and self-mastery.

Almost everyone knows how to integrate, at least to a degree. Most people, however, integrate around a false core. They integrate with their fears, doubts, and worries; their grievances, anger, and resentments; their cravings, fantasies, and wishes; power, sex, and money; or self-pity and victimhood. They end up neurotic and paranoid, instead of cheerful and well-balanced. In Jungian terms, they have integrated with the dark side of their character — instead of with the best within them.

The agent of light cannot afford these gaps in character. It is therefore important to learn as much as possible about the magical process of integration—and to use the tools we have at our disposal.

The problem with integrating a large part of our life around a negative force such as worry is that a strong emotion can be more addictive than alcohol or drugs. Worry, anger, fantasy, lust, or vengeance are negative forces with a life of their own. Once you bring them into your emotions, it is hard to expel them. They cling to their host like a parasite.

We must therefore see the wholesome wisdom of choosing only spiritual qualities and talents to include in the work of integration. We must integrate solely with the light and love of divine life, not with cheap thrills, negativity, or materialistic goals.

In other words, if we determine that we lack joyfulness in our character, we must recognize that we also lack attunement to spirit's inherent joy—and not seek joy by demanding that the circumstances of life must please us. We must dynamically increase the value we place on this inherent joy, and reform our character so that we begin to approach even the challenges and hardships of life with a wholesome cheerfulness and enthusiasm.

These new additions to our character become growing centers of enlightenment within us. To help the work of integration, they must be linked to the spiritual blueprint of the soul for our character and productivity. In this way, they create a channel for the integrative inclusiveness of spirit to flow from level to level into our daily acts and deeds.

In an earlier chapter, we defined five basic aspects of awareness we can use as centers of enlightenment:

1. A sense of spiritual identity.
2. Our values and beliefs.
3. Our priorities.
4. Our intentions.
5. Our awareness.

These core elements are the basis of the work of integration—the foundation on which we build. But it must be remembered that any of these elements can be used to harm us as easily as they can be used to help us. If we identify with an ethnic group instead of spirit, we can be trapped in the limitations of that group. If we believe that it is unimportant to grow, then we will make it almost impossible to mature in meaningful ways. If we feel compelled to help reform society, we may be responding to the plan of the soul—but we could be motivated just as easily by deep-seated antagonisms and rebelliousness.

It is therefore highly important to ensure that we undertake the work of integration under the supervision of spirit, lest we tear apart our character instead of making it whole. As long as our efforts are based in inclusiveness—the essence of integration—we should be able to make intelligent choices.

Fortunately, the design of human nature contains seven psychological tools that can be used to pursue the work of integration safely and wisely. Like any tool, these seven can be misused or misrepresented by someone bent on mischief. But when used by intelligent people in harmony with their basic spiritual design, they will prove most effective in accelerating the work of integration.

These seven tools of integration are:

1. Self-discipline. Everyone has some measure of self-discipline—at the very least, the ability to stay quiet while watching a movie. But many people do not use this skill to promote and support their highest purposes and goals. It would be like fixing an elaborate Thanksgiving dinner for twelve but forgetting to invite the guests—or serving each dish at a different time, instead of all at once. Self-disicpline is the means by which we stay on task and make sure that individual acts serve a common purpose. In the case of spiritual integration, it is the purpose of spirit that must be served first. Self-discipline links the work of integration with our values and goals, as well as our established priorities.

2. An ability to nurture growth. What is our purpose? What is the soul trying to promote? How do we translate it into activities? What resources do we need? How do we support and sustain this growth once it is launched? These are all questions that must be answered as we pursue the work of integrating spirit into our character.

In pursuing spiritual growth, for example, our goal is to achieve self-mastery, not just obtain additional knowledge and skills, or a greater capacity to relax. We might start the process of self-improvement with a lesser purpose, but once we shift gears and it becomes spiritual growth, our goal must become more inclusive. We are obliged to develop intelligent habits of self-examination and contemplation. We could, for instance, become more peaceful just by avoiding problems; we could become more efficient by abandoning duties. But we only nurture growth if we learn to act more persistently and skillfully in approaching these problems and duties. We need to tap and activate the inner substance of spirit, not just the outer appearance of spirituality.

The ability to nurture our growth with spiritual forces links us with purpose.

3. Innovation. Spiritual integration always results in the creation of something new in our life. So, we should ask: what do we need to discover? How can we look at old problems in new ways? What new spiritual resources do we need? What assumptions and limitations do we need to discard?

Most of the work of innovation is internal. We should therefore take inventory of what attitudes and beliefs need to be revised, what new habits need to be installed, and what new priorities need to be adopted. In a chronic illness, for example, we may have unwittingly fallen into a habit of resenting and fighting our symptoms, rather than working to build health. A subtle shift in motivation may be all that is needed to let spirit pour in and finish the healing.

Innovation links us more powerfully with the core element of awareness.

4. Transformation. The work of integration is not

as simplistic as switching from brand X to brand Y, and benefiting from the change. We must open ourself to new issues of spirit and learn to use them to transform our character and ability to act. It is counterproductive, for example, for a discouraged person to analyze and struggle endlessly with his or her depression. The only permanent solution is to align with the joy and enthusiasm of spirit and use them to transform his character and self-expression.

This can be a difficult transition for a person steeped in hopelessness. The personality tends to believe that only by fighting the hopelessness can it survive. In fact, it is just digging the pit of depression deeper and deeper. The tightness and grimness of the personality must be opened to the rising sun of spirit, and let its joy pour in.

The tool of transformation helps us connect more fully with our true sense of identity, establish healthier priorities, and focus our intention.

5. Knowledge and skill. Often, the greatest barrier to integration is our lack of understanding. We know about spirit, but view it one-dimensionally. We remain confused as to what it wants us to do—or how to proceed. This leads in many cases to the personality magnifying once again its sense that a huge gap exists between it and the soul.

Such perceptions are mostly illusory. We have probably spent our whole life learning about spirit and what it wants us to do—but have neglected to organize it in a coherent summary that we can understand. This is not the fault of spirit, which has all knowledge. It is a lack of skill on the part of the personality in digesting the guidance it has been given.

For this reason, we need to spend time reviewing the key lessons in living we have learned in this life. How has the soul helped us learn these new skills or insights? How did the message come through? How were we encouraged to practice and rehearse new habits, perspectives, or beliefs?

It is best to conduct this review before we have a desperate need to trust the soul or look to it for guidance. The tools of knowledge and skill help link us with the core elements of values and beliefs, priorities, and awareness.

6. Commitment. Without a fundamentally sound commitment to the life of spirit, the work of integration will be limited. Commitment is an indispensable ingredient in building a stronger connection with spirit. It must be a stable and reliable bridge between our active self and our highest self.

The lack of commitment often results in an excessive vulnerability to setbacks and failures. We may see our goals and their benefits clearly, yet still abandon our pursuit of them when we become discouraged. A strong commitment to worthwhile goals helps us restart ourself if we should falter. Our capacity for commitment empowers us by reconnecting us to the wellspring of spiritual purpose.

The tool of commitment helps us enrich the core elements of our priorities and intentions.

7. Conscience. One of the major ways in which we discover the existence of dys-integration within our char-

acter is through ethical struggles—where one principle clashes violently with another, or the habit of selfishness conflicts with our dedication to helpfulness. These are often very poignant conflicts.

The lack of conscience often exposes the inconsistencies of our behavior. We may be tolerant and charitable toward family members and friends, but unhelpful and unkind toward others. In this way, we betray a lack of conscience in how we interpret and apply the ideals of generosity and helpfulness.

The average worker in our society, for example, eagerly points out any hint of mistreatment of the work force by management, but seems totally indifferent to his or her own dishonesty in cutting corners or not paying attention to the work being done. These workers seem to view work as an insult, without any pangs of conscience that their own attitude sabotages the productivity of the company.

The tool of conscience helps keep the core elements of values and beliefs, priorities, and awareness connected into spirit.

The integration of new measures of spirit into our character and self-expression is a life-long process. It never ends. It is as important to our well-being and contentment as breathing. To sustain the work of integration, we must engage ourself in ongoing self-examination and the daily review and revision of our priorities, attitudes, and beliefs.

In other words, we must continue to *think*.

Integration is not an activity to postpone until we are

desperate. Our character is far too complex and vulnerable. If we work at integration erratically, or wait until we can put if off no longer, we are apt to achieve little but frustration and despair.

We never outgrow the need to grow. Growth is a fundamental impulse of the life of spirit. Nothing is more deadly in life than deciding we have grown enough. The work of integration, by contrast, keeps our options open—it creates new opportunities for us to expand our knowledge and skill.

The real threat to integration is arrogant smugness—the belief that "I know enough already." The person who decides that he or she has no need to learn or grow has committed psychological suicide.

Equally deadly is the attitude that "I can do no more. I am doing all that I can; life cannot ask me to do anything more." This sneaky attitude poisons many fine people on the spiritual path. It is a blend of self-absorption and rebellion masking an unwillingness to let spirit take control of their lives.

The antidote to these attitudes is a simple one: spirit. The essence of all integration is to include more and more of the life of spirit into our actual life—into our decision-making, our sense of identity, and our actions. As we pursue this work, we enrich ourself in new ways every day. Our character becomes a true launching pad for opportunity and achievement, integrated into the genius, compassion, and power of divine life.

In fact, this is the secret of integration. We may start out trying to cure a bad habit, but we end with a stronger vision of how to achieve self-mastery—a powerful reward for a small amount of effort.

It is easy to put the tools of integration to work in our life. We must simply examine our character and ask: where is there a notable inconsistency in our attitudes and habits? In other words, do we give in from time to time to flare-ups of anger, even though we want to be calm and loving? Do we brood and worry on a regular basis, even though we desire to trust in our spiritual self? Do we have hysterical reactions to life's events?

Whatever the inconsistency is, we must then focus on what quality of consciousness or element of divine life we need to embrace in order to eliminate it. If we worry, for example, this habit suggests that we lack the poise and certainty of spirit. If we become angry and reactive, we clearly need a stronger measure of the goodwill and tolerance of spirit.

Once we have identified the spiritual force needed, we must then work daily to activate this ideal and integrate it into our normal self-expression, by rehearsing the best way to respond in such circumstances in the future. We need to envision ourself accepting criticism with grace and an understanding response, rather than an angry, defensive reaction.

The final step, of course, is paying attention to our acts and deeds, to make sure our good intentions are translated into a new measure of goodwill and helpfulness—rather than revert to animosity and conflict.

By our fruits we shall be known.

5.

Integrating Conduct with Intentions

One of the primary ways that spiritual energies enter human expression is through the link between our good intentions and our habitual conduct. This is not an automatic avenue, however. If good intentions led instantly to wonderful achievements and results, the world would be a paradise—and our life would be a series of unbroken delights.

Clearly, this is not the case. We intend to lose weight, but we break our diet. We intend to clean out the closet, but the task remains undone. We intend to read the books we bought last year, but we do not. We want to become a better, more spiritual person, but we remain basically the same as before.

Our goals are clear and noble; our intentions are worthwhile. But we often fall short of enacting them. What is wrong?

Quite simply, we have failed to integrate two different aspects of our humanity: our intentions and our conduct. As a result, our daily behavior and activity may actually betray our best intentions and goals. At the very least, we fail to activate one of the strongest sources of action and strength within us, our intentions. We are unable to tap the rich power of spiritual motivation.

There are two instances when intentions always do lead to results: a) if we truly want to act, and b) if we absolutely must act. If we decide to quit smoking, for example, it will be relatively easy to do so, if we truly want to do so. But if we do not wish to quit, our efforts are doomed to fail—and we may even conclude that we are hopelessly addicted. Years later, however, when the doctor orders us to quit smoking after our second heart attack, we will find that we are able to do so—because we must.

This reality suggests a clue. We have a huge undeveloped potential to translate intentions into daily conduct, even though most people fail to do so more often than not. They do not fail because their intentions are weak; they fail because something vital is missing from the process: the skills of integration.

To put it in other terms, we do not know how to mobilize the power of motivation. We long for improvements in our life, but do not harness the power to act intelligently. In some instances, we give up after a few attempts and accept defeat as the best we can do. In other words, we never take the time to define clearly what our noble intentions are. At best, we end up just "going with the flow."

Most people, in fact, never see the link between intentions and conduct. They end up wandering through life as though it were a maze of bewildering choices. They hear the admonition "just do it!" and so they do, even though they have no idea what "it" is.

The failure to understand the importance of integrating daily behavior with noble intentions is a great personal tragedy, however. It undermines our sense of competence and thwarts our ability to achieve. We begin thinking of ourself as a "born loser."

This is not a healthy way to approach life. Spirit has designed us to be successful in life and content with our blessings and opportunities. If we start regarding ourself as a loser, we seriously impair our capacity to serve spirit. We create a breach in our connection between behavior and intention.

The good news is that this breach is relatively easy to repair. Unbeknownst to most people, spirit is heavily invested in the life of the personality. If we turn to spirit, we can harness the power of its motivation to strengthen the link between our intentions and our behavior.

Building and enriching this link between the personality and the soul is one of the primary functions of integration.

In playing golf, if we stand on the tee and swing at the ball without any clear motive, goal, or skills, the ball is apt to end up in a lake, in the rough, or the woods.

Our motive is to have fun, play as well as we can, be competitive with others, and complete the course. This motive defines the compelling reasons to begin this game, continue it, and finish. It gives us the strength we need to approach each shot with our best ability.

The goal will be different with each stroke. We must pick a precise target and focus our attention on hitting the ball to it. This target must not be a negative one—as in trying to miss a bunker—lest our focus of attention direct the ball toward the very hazard we hope to miss! Our target should therefore be the middle of the fairway or the center of the green, as dictated by the kind of shot we are making. We must also remember that the goal for each stroke is always to minimize the total number of shots needed to put the ball in the hole.

Our level of skill determines the way we approach each shot. We need not only the ability to swing the club, but also the knowledge to pick the right club and the best strategy for using it. Hitting the ball well requires more than just motor skills—it also demands concentration, so that we transmit our intention to put the ball in the cup to our subconscious, which then controls our swing so that we come as close to the cup as possible.

In actually hitting the ball, we must do so with supreme confidence in our skills and concentration. Any hesitation will break our concentration and lead to topped and shanked balls.

When we have poor swings, it is not because the process of aligning our skills with our goal and our motive has failed; it is because we have let ourself be distracted. Perhaps we are intimidated by our opponent, or more preoccupied with failing than with hitting the ball cleanly.

In any event, we are the obstacle that prevents us from expressing our skill level appropriately.

The same template can be applied to any effort to translate our intentions into our habits and conduct. We must focus on building a high quality, strong motive; we must establish effective goals; and we must prepare ourself to act with knowledge and skills.

Our motives must be:

• Clear, not mixed. Some ill people want to get well, but are reluctant to give up the indulgence of being cared for by others. This mixed motive blocks their healing efforts.

• Compelling. Our motive must be strong enough to drive us to act, subconsciously as well as consciously. It must be a top priority in our life, so that we become strong enough to defeat resistance.

• Constant. It is easy to start any reform with a strong burst of enthusiasm. It is more difficult to remain true to a goal or objective during days of temptation and difficulty. We must therefore establish a constant mindfulness of our motivation.

• Correct. We must forge our motives out of spirit, not negative reactiveness. Anger or revenge may be strong impelling forces, but they are not ones that will be supported by spirit. They are therefore incorrect under any circumstances. Our motives must be based on achievement, not destruction.

Our goals must be:

• Concrete. We cannot afford to be vague or sub-jective; we must know when we have achieved our goal.

A goal of being "a good person" or "doing the right thing" may orient us in the right direction, but it may be too general to stir up right action. By contrast, a goal such as "treating other people with respect and dignity" is focused and concrete. We will know when we have succeeded in implementing our goal—and when we have failed. In this way, we translate our noble intent more effectively.

Many people who work hard at growing but never feel as if they achieve anything simply have set goals that are excessively vague.

• Achieveable. Many spiritual aspirants harm themselves by setting goals that are far too ambitious. Then, when they find it difficult to achieve their goals, they react negatively to their "failure." This weakens their confidence and interferes with other efforts to grow.

• Constructive. When we find ourself in the midst of controversy or difficulty, it is always easiest to point out what is wrong and demand that it be stopped. Often, this casts us immediately in the role of "opposition"—and our ideas are met with suspicion and antagonism. It is usually far wiser to offer to assist and support ongoing efforts than it is to protest and oppose.

• Compatible—with the designs and plans of our higher self. If our higher self is guiding us to act patiently and tolerantly, for example, it would be silly to set a goal that would force us to compete ruthlessly with others.

We must then take steps to acquire whatever skills or wisdom we need in order to reach our goal. An artist, obviously, would need to study art and refine his skills.

But some of the attributes we need to acquire may not be so apparent.

Although many people make the assumption that they know enough, artists and geniuses do not; they continue learning throughout their entire life. In part, this is what differentiates them from ordinary achievers.

This principle applies to problems that are thrust upon us as well. A person who contracts cancer will probably set the goal of getting well. But what does getting well truly mean? In the case of cancer, the physical illness is almost always the embodiment of an underlying, emotional cancer—a pessimistic belief system, perhaps, or a long-standing habit of chronic hostility. The best goal to set in such a case is to cleanse and purify these negative attitudes and destructive emotions—not just get well. So we need to build skills in enriching the quality of our emotions.

As we gain experience in integrating specific intentions into constructive achievements and changes in our life, we can then come to appreciate that this work is but the first stage in a larger activity—the work of spiritualizing the whole breadth of our conduct and character. While it is a great step forward for a nasty or cynical person to see through his self-imposed limitations and start to replace them with new and better habits, such a personality still falls far short of being an enlightened companion of the soul. We must therefore understand that the work of integrating our behavior and conduct with the intentions of the soul must be an ever-expanding process.

It may be enough for the average person to fulfill his or her duties as a parent, a citizen, and a thinking adult—but it would not be enough for the agent of light. In fact, fulfilling these duties would be only a starting point. The agent of light is expected to fulfill his duties as a spiritual person as well. Often, these duties are very much different from the obligations of the personality.

In this case, it is not enough to be integrated with our good intentions. We must also be integrated with the plan and guidance of the soul. We must accept the soul's greater wisdom—and be content with the opportunities it hands us.

The process remains the same; it is just linked to a higher pattern of intention.

• Our motives become rooted in our will to grow and serve. We become impelled by our love of life and an inner urge to be helpful and constructive.

• Our goals stop being focused on achieving fame or wealth or even health and become refocused on purifying the emotions, enlightening the mind, and mastering our approach to life so that our efforts truly serve the soul.

• Our skills and knowledge become more subtle and sublime. We develop intuitive skills that will help connect us more fully with the intelligence of spirit. We master skills of thinking and reason and learn to manage failure, rejection, loss, and disappointment. We become aware of a growing ability to recollect who we truly are, no matter what external circumstances or timing try to tell us. We learn, above all, to transcend our worries and wounds and to take effective steps to heal them.

This higher level of integration lets us "prepare the way" for becoming an inspired agent of light.

Any motive, goal, or skill can be used as a starting point for integrating our behavior with our intentions—for example, for examining our commitment to the life of spirit.

To start, we must define our idea of enlightenment. Do we view it as something that will enrich the life of the personality—or do we see it in terms of enabling the soul to express itself through our life?   Have we made this commitment, in other words, for the good of the soul or the good of the personality. If it is the former, we will be able to harness the motives of spirit.   If the latter, we will continue to be stuck largely in the motives of materialism.

What are our goals in achieving enlightenment? Are we striving for perfection—or are we striving to become the best person we can be?   If we strive for perfection, we have embraced a false goal; no matter how much we grow, we will always be somewhere less than perfect! If we strive to be an honest, wise, and tolerant person, however, we have set specific targets we can reach.

In making this inspection, of course, we may find that our goals are far less noble than we thought them to be.   Perhaps we have turned to the light of the soul primarily to fill the drab emptiness of our life. We will then be apt to set our goals in such a way that they feed our fantasies and wish life, rather than a true hunger for spiritual nutrition.

Next, we must truthfully evaluate the skills we must acquire and the wisdom we must develop in order to reach enlightenment. These will include training the mind to respond to archetypal realities and control the reactiveness of the emotions and physical urges. It will also include learning to look at the world around us more globally—with greater detachment and impersonality.

Finally, we can judge the quality and strength of our commitment. Is it compelling, clear, consistent, and correct? How can it be expanded? In what ways do we still fall short of the ideal?

In this way, we learn that, in order for enlightenment to unfold, we must set the table for it. We must do our best to link our motives, goals, and skills with our capacity to act. In this way, we gradually cause a strong bond to develop between spirit and our personality. As a result, the work of integration proceeds—step by step.

6.

Integrating the Emotions with the Mind

One of the most divisive conflicts we can experience is the internal war that arises whenever the mind and the emotions compete with each other for control of our decision-making capacity. This competition is a very common occurrence. It arises in the individual who knows he should be tolerant, yet at the same time yearns to get even with supposed enemies. It likewise can be found in the person who needs to dominate others, even though he knows he often embarrasses himself in the process. It can also occur in the person who feels insecure, even though he knows that the facts do not justify this feeling. Such competition is a certain sign that we have not effectively integrated the mind and the emotions, so they will work harmoniously together.

Other signs that the mind and emotions are not

properly integrated include unstable moods, inconsistent thinking, and unbalanced behavior. These are all examples of extreme thoughts and emotions being allowed to operate unchecked.

Some people, for example, are shameless in the way they gush emotionally over a new idea that appeals to them; a week later, they have forgotten all about it. Other individuals are harshly critical and judgmental of everything and everyone—or move through life in a chronic fog of depression. In each of these instances, neither the mind nor the emotions is able to correct or restrain the unbalanced behavior of the other.

A third problem indicating a lack of integration between the mind and the emotions arises when the emotions try to control the mind or, more rarely, when the mind tries to subjugate the emotions. A prejudiced person, for example, may use the mind to justify the preservation of his or her hostility. A phobic individual may likewise seek out reasons to justify his or her fears. But the reverse is also true: many people who are trapped in ideology will use the emotions to support their limited views. This is true of fundamentalist Christians who claim that their condemnations of other Christians are "acts of love."

We cannot afford to let these gaps fester in our personality, lest we end up disconnecting our mind from our emotions entirely. The mind and the emotions are the two great forces of our personal self-expression. We are meant to nurture them and help both of them become more and more mature. At the same time, we are expected to help them learn to work cooperatively with each other. This is the work of integration.

Let it be clearly understood: there is an enormous difference between mature emotions and immature ones; between a mature mind and an immature mind.

The immature emotions tend to be self-centered, in need of constant pampering and indulgence. They are regularly drenched in self-pity and victimhood, blaming life or others for their problems. They are reactive to life, and therefore vulnerable to fear, worry, grief, and anger. They personalize everything.

The immature mind tends to be narrow in its focus, full of doubt and criticism. It has a hard time grasping the larger picture (the abstract view) of any situation. It may well identify more with rationalizations than with understanding.

Mature emotions, by contrast, are capable of embracing the qualities of God, life, our highest self, and other people. They can be highly sensitive to the needs of life and others, as well as responsive to spirit. But this sensitivity is directed at the sublime currents of life, not the dense wish life of mass consciousness or emotionally-based individuals.

Our emotions can learn the lessons of maturity by learning to encourage and support our colleagues, not criticize or reject them; by learning to act gracefully and calmly in life, rather than become irritated; by learning to act cheerfully, even when the circumstances of life are threatening.

The mature mind has the capacity to embrace the knowledge of God, the soul, and the plan for our life.

It observes and discerns what is true and accurate, comprehends it, and then organizes our talents and skills to build toward our goals.

Our mind learns the lessons of maturity by linking itself with the reservoir of knowable things in the mind of God and learning to apply the insights and guidance found at these spiritual levels to the practical challenges of daily living. It learns to express these new realizations with self-control, consistency, and thoroughness.

Both of these vehicles of our self-expression will function best when they are used together, in harmony with each other. Indeed, the soul has designed us to learn to use our emotions as a mature companion of the mind—and to use the two of them together as an enlightened companion of spirit. Achieving this level of integration is a fundamental requirement of the agent of light.

When the mature emotions are integrated with a mature mind, and the two of them together are enlightened by spirit, a wonderful transformation takes place in our consciousness. Our faith is strengthened by knowledge. Our talents and skills can be expressed with enthusiasm. Our wisdom can protect us from naïveté and gullibility. Gentleness enables us to correct others and ourself without offending. Charity enables us to work for justice without becoming arrogant or righteous.

As this integration occurs, the gaps and great divides within our character close up and become healed. Both the emotions and the mind move steadily toward serving a common purpose:

Enlightenment.

In pursuing the integration of our mind and emotions, we need to understand a few key points:

1. As the greater meets the lesser, the greater is always designed to absorb and improve the lesser. There is absolutely no point, in other words, in trying to integrate anger or grief with anything. Nor is there any value in attempting to integrate stupidity or bias with anything. An imperfect or immature thought or feeling must be transformed into something more mature before we can successfully integrate it with spirit. Anger must be replaced by tolerance; grief must be washed away by the essence of contentment.

2. It is therefore necessary to cultivate a level of detached self-awareness that will make it possible to examine our thoughts and emotions objectively—as well as control and reorient them. As long as we are unable to see that our thoughts and emotions are working at cross purposes, for example, we will not be capable of teaching them to work cooperatively. As long as we fail to understand that our reactive patterns are rebelling against the higher intentions of the soul, we will not be able to harness the power of integration.

It is not easy to rein in and control an emotional tendency to become hysterical whenever we experience a minor setback. Nor is it easy to understand how commonly our thoughts are captured and directed by outside influences, be it an ethnic group mind or a domineering spouse. Nonetheless, we must learn to recognize and control such tendencies, or they will end up taking hostage any effort to integrate.

3. Our goal must be maturity, both in the emotions and in the mind. The emotions can be used in silly, childish ways—to express anger, self-pity, fear, worry, or grief. The mind can likewise be used in silly, childish ways—to deny truth, to rationalize our failings, to perpetuate superstition, and so on. If the process of integration is going to work for us, we must first give up our childish ways and begin acting like an adult, both emotionally and mentally. We must not glorify the inner child, but rather embrace our potential to be a noble adult. Only the adult potential within our thoughts and feelings is able to attract a response from spirit. Childish, immature elements quickly repel the interest of spirit.

4. For the mind and the emotions to work together, we must clearly define the role of each of these vehicles—and how they can best work together. The primary work of the emotions is to add quality to any activity. The primary work of the mind is to understand and supervise our activities. It should therefore be clear that the emotions reach the apex of their expressiveness when intelligently controlled and guided by an enlightened mind.

People who are mired in their emotions may not like these suggestions, but they are valid. The mind, working under the enlightened guidance of the soul, can select the ideal mood we should be expressing far better than the emotions. In a crisis, undisciplined emotions are apt to opt for hysteria and panic. The detached mind, on the other hand, may see that a mood of calmness and endurance is a more constructive option.

5. We need to redefine the roles of our emotions and

mind in the context of maturity, thereby discovering the larger purpose of our activities. If we are a parent, for example, we should begin to view the emotions as a noble instrument for nurturing our children with love and the mind as a perfect tool for revealing to our children the patterns and principles of divine life. If we use emotions to humiliate our children or the mind to teach them pessimistic and cynical habits, we end up perpetuating the cycle of immaturity—and will be ill-equipped for the work of integration.

Once the emotions and mind learn to work together in this way, they become a powerful combination for self-expression. Until then, however, they may well produce more mischief than constructive help.

We do not pursue the work of integration by attacking immature behavior directly, however. We look for the inner assumptions—the seeds—from which conflicting or destructive behavior springs. By changing these matrices deep within our character, we then clear the way for the integration of the mind and the emotions to occur.

A good example is provided by victims of childhood abuse. These people may be very bright, with a good education, loving spouses, and a good job. Yet they are tyrannized by an evil plot in the emotions and the mind to perpetuate the pain and suffering of childhood indefinitely, as they continue to react to events from thirty or forty years in the past. Even worse, they continually reinvent this childhood trauma as adults, by justifying every resentment and insult they experience in terms of these earlier events. This makes recovery all but impossible—until they start asking the right kind of questions.

The first question to ask is: what is the purpose in believing themselves to be victims? It is clear that they were victims forty years ago, but how does this apply to today? Are they dedicated to perpetuating pain and misery? Are they helped by hating their parents forever? Is it their goal to be the greatest martyr in the state? Do they love to wallow in self-pity?

Next, they need to ask: are these belief patterns consistent with getting well? The answer, of course, will be "no." The path to inner peace is not found in the midst of constant irritation. The path to goodwill is not found by blaming others. The path to liberation is not found in continuously reliving the threats of the past.

This leads then to a third question: how do these earlier memories corrupt current thoughts and feelings? They are using the mind to justify a lifetime as a victim, wearing their suffering on their sleeves, tantamount to a permanent "pass" on all future tests. They are furthermore using the emotions to magnify the importance of these former hurts and threats. Instead of taking constructive steps to heal them and move beyond them, they let their memories remain mired in the quicksand of abuse.

Whenever the emotions and mind are twisted and corrupted by such an effort to preserve the misery of the past, all efforts to integrate with spirit will fail—until the individual reverses direction and sees how much his or her sense of identity has been warped, not as a child but as an adult!

As a result, the ability to cope with life is poisoned by blame and anger, rather than nurtured with goodwill.

The ability to think about life has been ravaged by resentment for what has happened, instead of focused on the good opportunities that lie ahead.

The meaning of the past has been skewed to the point where it has become an irrational specter that cannot be defeated.

But it can be defeated, because the specter is just an illusion—an illusion they have created and sustained. If these people can disassemble the specter they have built, and see how it has fed a whole empire of thoughts and feelings, then they can heal themselves. They can learn to put the past behind them, and move forward.

Not all of us suffer from such extreme trauma, of course, but this example serves as a good model for any effort to integrate the mind and the emotions.

We must start with the assumption that our purpose is to heal ourself and work toward wholeness. We must also recognize that our greatest key for success lies in harnessing the healing presence and wisdom of spirit. We can then turn the unlimited power of this presence on four key seeds or matrices of consciousness:

Our sense of identity. We are a divine being with a healthy design for wholeness. This design is never corrupted by any trauma that afflicts us. It is always whole, and therefore always has the power to help us triumph over any adversity. It even has the power to help us learn how we have been immeasurably enriched by the misfortune and setbacks we may have suffered. For this reason, it is practical to shift our sense of identity from being a victim of life, helpless and abandoned, to being a survivor who has adequate resources to take charge of life now.

Our coping style. Instead of blaming others for our problems but doing nothing about them, we can change our moods and expectations and triumph over the problems that have long entrapped us. Instead of feeling sorry for ourself, we can strengthen our emotions with hope and aspiration. Instead of retreating from challenge, we can charge the mind with a strong will to restart our life. We can direct the mind to look for constructive options and repair any damage we may have done, to others or to ourself.

Our thinking style. Our mind must become more and more saturated with a growing respect for our potential and our future. We must dwell on the reasons why we can succeed and triumph in life, rather than endlessly analyzing our failures and losses. We need to reinterpret the meaning of the events of life as lessons not insults, as steps in our learning process of building health and maturity.

Our personal style. Too many of us use the emotions to magnify threats, worries, and deficiencies. We need to teach the emotions to do the reverse: to magnify the best and noble elements in our life and personality, while harnessing the light of the soul to shrink the scope of our problems. We need to reorient our feelings so that they support our opportunities for change, our growing awareness of spirit, our resources, and our survival skills—and to register and rejoice in what we have accomplished in this life. We also need to teach the emotions that their primary job is to enrich our life with cheerfulness, our work with enthusiasm, relations with goodwill, and aspirations with faith and reverence.

As we focus on each of these areas, our intent must be to create and nurture healthy new seeds we can then use to replace the unhealthy and immature seeds we have gleaned from earlier "harvests" the harvests of woe and malaise from prior experiences in life. We must work with intelligent love as well as loving intelligence to make these wonderful changes—changes that will enable us to express our highest good more fully.

A good exercise for learning how to integrate the mind and the emotions more fully begins with selecting a situation where the outcome is not matching our expectations.

As we review this situation, we realize that something is out of line—and it may well be ourself. In any event, we should resist the temptation to blame others while we try to go beyond the present circumstance and define the larger purpose. What is spirit trying to teach or show us?

Once we have defined this basic issue, the next question is: where is this learning process breaking down? How have we misinterpreted the right way to:

- Feel.
- Think.
- Act.

Where does a conflict between the mind and the emotions—or between ourself and spirit—keep us focused in conflict and pettiness? How can we rise above these distortions?

Trying to be as detached as possible, we also need to ask: what is the best way to think and feel about this situation? What would be the ideal resolution? What is the best way to achieve such a resolution? What are we doing to obstruct a solution?

Finally, we need to examine what it means to magnify the ideal way to feel and think. How can we enrich our constructive feelings and thoughts with the greater presence of spirit? What new matrices or seeds should we create to guide us through the years ahead?

7.

Integrating Ideas with Ideals

The human mind is designed to work with ideas. Many people think that all ideas originate in the mind, because they are not aware of being impressed mentally by independent stimuli. But ideas that "originate" in our own mind tend to reflect our recollection of personal experience, our reaction to what others think about us, our recognition of cultural traditions, and other simplistic concepts. The mind, in short, becomes trapped in a small world of its own invention.

It behooves the agent of light, therefore, to seek out greater sources to inspire and motivate his or her thinking. In making this search, however, we must rise above the cleverly-disguised desires and wants of wishful thinking, the rigid patterns of peer pressure, and the ideologies of unthoughtful people. It is no gain to fill the mind with beliefs and opinions and expectations that lower our understanding of life!

Instead, we need to understand that the intent of the soul, when it comes to the matter of thinking, is that we learn to link our personal ideas with spiritual Ideals.

These Ideals are the "standards" of human behavior and design, as defined by the soul. An example of a spiritual Ideal would be joy. The soul has designed us to enjoy life, drink deeply of its opportunities, and express ourself with èlan and grace. But very few people have learned to attune their mind to the abstract force of spiritual joy, which is the soul's response to life. Instead, they reach instinctively for the satisfaction of personal desire—happiness—but find it fleeting and hard to hold. They fall short of the Ideal, and stumble through life largely devoid of joy.

This sad state of spiritual emptiness is not part of our spiritual design! It is what occurs by default when we make no effort to discover spiritual ideals and imbue our thinking with them. Sometimes, our lack of responsiveness to spirit is merely the result of ignorance. At other times, it is the result of arrogance—we haughtily decide that we will create our own standards for living, and substitute them for the genuine article, spiritual ideals. In either case, the end is the same: we deprive ourself of the essence and delight of human living—the presence of spirit!

The average person, of course, is not accustomed to working with these ideals—nor focusing the mind upon them and building a harmonious rapport with them. Most people are stuck in the morass of mundane activities. If they think at all, their ideas are heavily tinged with pessimism and shortsightedness. They lack imagination, content to try to endure life without trying to enrich or improve it. In such people, the "standard" stands no longer for excellence and triumph; it is a signal, instead, that they have become comfortable with the mediocre. In the end, it cuts off opportunity and traps them in a shell of their own making.

Agents of light, by contrast, must deal with all the same mundane problems, but they sense that there must be a better way than the commonplace. They are impelled by a vision of excellence and nobility. And, in most cases, they find it!

These people have learned the power of focusing on a spiritual ideal and integrating it into the ideas and values that shape and drive their daily lives. In many cases, they probably do not recognize the ideal as "spiritual"; but, if it lifts them up to the level of the abstract principles of enlightened living, it is. If, as they learn to express it, it enriches their lives and deepens their wisdom, it is.

Many people are learning to attune the mind to the spiritual Ideal in only one or two important areas of life. The agent of light, however, takes the process even further. Instead of being inspired and driven by excellence in one or two key areas of life, we universalize the effort. We view the soul as the source of all spiritual ideals, and focus our innate curiosity on learning to connect with these ideals in every facet of life. We teach ourself to tap the power and motivation of these ideals, and integrate them seamlessly into our thoughts, values, principles, attitudes, and behavior. In this way, we transform our character and behavior; we bring heaven to earth.

This is the task of integrating ideas with Ideals.

As we approach the realm of spiritual Ideals, we must take great care to associate only with the genuine article. There are a lot of petty and destructive notions that masquerade as ideals. One is vanity. It is found in teenage girls who want to be thinner than anyone else. It is found in men who want more money, a bigger house, and so on. Another is obsession. We become obsessed with exacting vengeance for real and imagined hurts; we become obsessed with guilt because we made some horrible mistake years ago; or we become obsessed with fear, and end up doing nothing and becoming nothing, just playing it safe. Fanaticism is yet another false ideal, leading to the worship of a chosen ideal with great enthusiasm, but little interest in constructive efforts to improve life. A similar problem is "magical thinking"—the expectation that spiritual ideals will work all by themselves, without any effort exerted on our part.

The difference between the agent of light who is integrated with spiritual Ideals and the average person who is not is enormous. Anyone can display a bumper sticker reading "Envision World Peace" or "Honk if you love Jesus." Genuine peace, however, demands that we learn how to act peacefully in our dealings with others. The love of Jesus must take root as a growing compassion and respect for our fellow human beings. Anything less falls short of the standard.

Spiritual Ideals have been forged in the mind of God. They are not products of human thinking. They are, instead, the *standards* for human thinking—the bar that we are meant to aspire to in our own daily conduct. In other words, if we aspire to joy, we must stand ready to become a joyful person in all that we do. It is not enough to say that we cherish joy, but then act with melancholy, moodiness, and pessimism.

How do we know if we have tapped a genuine spiritual Ideal? The answer is simpler than it may seem. The Ideal will be filled with archetypal power! As it enters our awareness, therefore, it will elevate our thinking, enrich our emotions, and vivify our physical presence. We will become a better person, empowered to solve problems and transcend the misery of human life. The plan of the soul will take root in our life and flourish. In addition, our relationships with others will improve.

The key to aligning ourself with spiritual Ideals is to combine an active curiosity with constructive speculation. Acting on the premise that there has to be something better than this, we need to learn to use our curiosity to explore questions such as: How does the soul view this obstacle or challenge? What can we do to improve our attitudes, understanding, and behavior?

To succeed, we need to approach these Ideals with an undying enthusiasm for pushing back the boundaries of the mind. We must be willing to question what we have been taught and what we have assumed. We have to make room in our mental household for spirit—and its Ideals.

The task of making room in our mind for the Ideals of spirit begins by disconnecting the tendency of the mind to run on "automatic pilot"—to be absorbed in worries, fears, trivial expectations, and the "background noise" of daily life. While doing household chores, for example, many people let their minds be filled with anxieties, idle speculations, fantasies, assumptions, and depressing or pessimistic notions. We must break this chain of thought and replace it with a conscious effort to fill our mind with joy, peace, harmony, affection, and a sense of beauty. We must learn to dwell on one or more of these Ideals whenever our mind would otherwise "idle."

Golfers know the value of making this kind of choice. If they approach a shot with a strong awareness of the need to stay out of a sand trap, they will drop their shot into the heart of the trap nine times out of ten. They cannot afford to let the mind be focused on potential mistakes; they must carefully direct all of their attention on the shot they intend to make, instead of the ways it may misfire.

This process calls for a new approach to thinking—a need to think before we think! We must build a habit of ascertaining the perfect spiritual Ideal to guide us in any proposed activity—then fill our mind with the abstract life of this Ideal before we start to examine the issue before us. While vacuuming, for example, we might develop a mental habit of contemplating purity and order as we engage in this chore. By filling our mind with purity and order, we make it easier to rise above the petty worries and fantasies that would otherwise afflict our idle mind.

This approach works with an occupied as well as an idle mind, of course. If we are a faultfinding, hypercritical person, we need to break our bad habit of focusing on what is wrong before it becomes possible to focus on what is correct. We need to cultivate an enthusiasm for celebrating what is good and useful about life. Then, when we are confronted with a problem, instead of launching into instant criticism, we can ask instead: "What is there about this situation that is good and deserves my support? How can I harness the spiritual Ideal to nourish the potential good in this situation?"

Like attracts like. If we are filled with a faultfinding mentality, we will attract more problems to us than opportunities. Far worse, we will be unable to attract the forces and qualities of spirit that nurture and support growth. After all, why would these ideals want to support our negativism?

As we learn to work in these ways with spiritual ideals, we set the stage for the transformation of our values, principles, and attitudes. We also become a more powerful force for change within society. In short, we develop a strong tie with the higher self. We stop viewing spirit as something antagonistic to daily affairs, and begin seeing how easy—and enriching—it is to express spirit in all that we do. In turn, this transformation brings to us a new measure of optimism about life. Our thinking matures in a number of key ways:

Our standards become higher. Instead of accepting a mediocre level of behavior and performance in our life, we become more directly involved in making our life work. We see opportunities to enrich life and we seize them, instead of just settling for mere survival, day by day. We learn to involve ourself and take worthwhile risks, instead of being passive and not making any waves. We begin to appreciate the vast difference between the absence of vice and the presence of virtue—the absence of hardship versus the expression of spiritual peace and joy. We also learn to honor our individual genius.

Our expectations become more constructive. Being in touch with spiritual ideals, we have a clearer understanding of what spirit expects in every situation. By attuning our expectations to those of spirit, our goals become more positive and, when achieved, more fulfilling. As a result, we become more optimistic than before, knowing as we do that our efforts are supported by spirit. We also tap a much more profound measure of worthiness. We learn what ideas are worthy, because they support the plans of spirit, and which are unworthy, because they lead us into the depths of materialism.

We rearrange our priorities. Instead of the comfort of the personality, we become more attuned to the willingness of spirit to accept some hardship and take on new responsibilities in order to achieve spiritual goals. In lieu of our personal convenience, we become more willing to innovate and act boldly. In the place of security, we become more willing to try new experiences and venture into new dimensions—even to look at ideas from new perspectives. Instead of approval, we become willing to endure some criticism and opposition, because our internal moral compass shows us the need to do so. In place of just getting by, we strive to honor the highest and the best. In lieu of following the herd, we learn to follow our own inner sense of direction and purpose.

We redefine "achievement." We begin to define our triumphs and accomplishments in terms of fulfilling the plans of the soul, rather than in terms of gratifying the needs of the personality. We hold ourself accountable for producing results—results that transform the quality or conduct of human life. We focus less on what we are doing and more on the impact it has in guiding humanity in intelligent directions.

Our habits mature. As we learn to steady our focus of attention in the ideals of spirit, our capacity to concentrate the mind expands. The clarity of our thought deepens; we learn to discern between a spiritual ideal on the one hand and its emotional reflection on the other. We become more self-starting than before, because now we are motivated by the force of spirit. Other key habits improve as well, as our ideas and values become tied more and more to the true source of inspiration: spirit.

Our beliefs enrich us. A belief in doom weakens our character and makes us vulnerable. A belief in the power of spirit to nurture and protect us, by contrast, helps us learn to rely on the strength of the higher life. To be an idealist, we must believe that life is good—filled with possibilities, support, and beauty. This basic linkage is of great importance, for the work of the agent of light exposes us to pessimism, depression, and the threat of defeat. Without our belief in spiritual Ideals, we will not be able to transform or redeem any of these pockets of darkness, in ourself, in others, or in society.

Most people entertain the pessimistic thought that they cannot make a difference. As a result, they withdraw into a protective shell and busy themselves "tending their own garden." Once we connect with the ideals of spirit, however, and learn to interact fully with them, everything changes. We know that a single person, interacting with the life of God, can indeed make a difference. We become aware of the plan guiding human development, and find our niche in it. We also begin to understand that life is designed to bless and enrich us—all of us.

Ultimately, we learn that each of us, individually and collectively, is worthy of these rich blessings.

This newfound sense of worthiness helps us recreate ourself and define a new identity for our time on earth. We become more profoundly aware of the opportunities that will let us "play our part with stern resolve." We begin to see ourself as something more than an agent of beauty or compassion or wisdom or harmony; we become the incarnation of the spiritual ideal! In other words, we become an expression of joy—or wisdom or harmony or compassion—on earth. More and more, we let the ideal we serve guide us and define us. In this way, heaven comes to earth.

Ultimately, we define who we are as a co-creator, with God, of what we are. We become the inspired author of our possibilities, the chief executive of our nobility, creativity, and excellence. We learn how powerfully we can shape our own experiences—and how to harness the ideals of spirit to mold our life's events constructively and creatively.

At the same time, our relationship with God deepens. We discover that God created us in order that we might become an agent of divine light.   By removing the barriers of ignorance and selfishness that have separated us from God, we fulfill this design.

Eventually, we must learn to relate to all spiritual ideals in this fashion.   At first, it may seem to be more than enough to become an agent of joy or harmony or wisdom.   But any one quality alone is not enough to complete our assignment on earth.   We must discover and learn to interact with all of the spiritual ideals that govern humanity.

We are designed to become an agent of Light.

To learn to integrate our ideas with these spiritual ideals, we select a habit, belief, or attitude that is handicapping our life.   It calls out for transformation.   This trait might be pessimism, faultfinding, guilt, apathy, or an abiding sense of worthlessness.

It should be a trait that dominates our thinking whenever the mind is idling.

We begin by challenging this characteristic. How does it damage us? How does it handicap our self-expression? How does it control us?   What does it cheat us from enjoying?   How have we rationalized or justified the damage it has done?

Then we need to ponder: what spiritual ideal would

heal this tendency, if we introduced it into our awareness? What do I know about this Ideal? How can I focus on it? How must I change my thinking?

It is at this point that the work of alignment must begin. We must make a habit of dedicating ourself to this Ideal whenever possible, especially filling our awareness with it when our mind is on idle—as in doing our chores, driving the car, daydreaming, and so on. The act of focusing the mind on this Ideal is all that is necessary at this stage. We do not need to strain; we just need to be persistent.

Once we have achieved a measure of alignment, we need to begin the work of interacting with this Ideal. We need to use the force and design of this Ideal to transform our habits, attitudes, and beliefs, so that they become infused with the ideal and actually express it.

The work of transforming a habit is an ongoing one requiring months, possibly years. As we make a routine of interacting with a spiritual Ideal, it seeps into every level of our subconscious and unconscious structures of character. In this way, we activate our own potential to express this Ideal.

We stand on the threshold of becoming a new person.

8.

Integrating the Body with Its Purpose

In Greek mythology, a centaur is a fabulous creature in which the upper half is man and the lower half is horse. It is said that the centaurs were the progeny of Ixion, king of Thessaly, and a cloud—the cloud being the goddess Hera, sent to Ixion by Zeus as a trick. But Ixion saw through the disguise and made love to Hera, enraging Zeus all the more.

The centaur is a powerful symbol for human consciousness. The upper half—spirit—is meant to control the lower half—the threefold personality of body, emotions, and mind. But in the human being, this control cannot occur until all three elements of the lower half have been integrated with the life of spirit.

To many people, the proposition of integrating the physical body with spirit is as unlikely as the report that

Ixion sired the centaurs by mating with a cloud! How can the dense physical body possibly integrate with the abstract life of spirit?

This riddle is puzzling only from the point of view of the personality. It is an open book to the soul, which knows that the physical body is a vehicle that can be trained. Left to its own devices, the body will be directed and driven by its addiction to cravings, fantasies, and urges. However, it can be trained to perform many athletic feats and mechnical skills. In the same way, the body can be trained to become responsive to the design and direction of spirit. When this occurs, then the upper half of the human being—consciousness—controls the lower half—sensation—and a new being emerges. Until it happens, however, the individual human being remains trapped in the physical form, a victim of his or her own immaturity and experience. The two halves of the human whole remain separated—divided, unable to fulfill its destiny.

For this reason, the agent of light perceives the importance of integrating the body with its spiritual design, even if the personality protests. Since it is not possible literally to integrate our kneecap with joy or peace, we must find another way. We must stop giving top priority to physical comfort and pleasure, and redefine our effort in terms of spirit. We must stop thinking about what we do not have and cannot do and start thinking in terms of what we can accomplish—plus our potential for even greater things!

The answer is found in the "cloud" of our spiritual design.

In all too many people, the urges and conditions of the physical body are impediments to spirit. We let our focus of attention be dominated and controlled by these factors, instead of learning to exercise control over them.

Nowhere is this condition more obvious than in the way we let our appetites and physical urges dominate our life. A great many people struggle with addictions to food, alcohol, ciagrettes, or drugs. In our modern era, when underweight models are hailed as the epitome of beauty and health, many women struggle also with anorexia and bulemia—in the name of physical fitness. Some people become addicted to sex—or allow a sexual orientation to control their lives and actions. Others become addicted to the needs for hugs and other superficial expressions of affection and comfort.

But it is not just appetites and addictions that we let control us. All too many people are tyrannized by their state of health. We have been taught that "if you have your health, you have everything." This maltruism misleads many people to place their physical vitality and comfort above every other consideration—and let fatigue and poor health interfere with their intent to serve spirit. It also causes people to emphasize physical regimens—diet and exercise, for example—as far more important than contact with spirit. They fail to comprehend that health emerges from spirit, not from jogging, vitamins, and fruit juice.

Physical handicaps and limitations also frequently cripple our capacity to integrate with spirit. The physical difficulty or constriction becomes the central absorbing problem of life—and spirit is pushed away, as something too distant to be relied on for relief. In fact, spirit contains the power to help us overcome and even eliminate most of these handicaps, but not when it is instantly relegated to a subordinate status, so that we can "deal" with our limitation!

For many people, especially spiritual aspirants, the great physical struggle is with inertia and fatigue. The mind, inspired by spirit, may lay out energetic, sweeping plans, but may be overwhelmed by the reluctance of the body to enact them. We know what we want to do, but we never quite get around to starting! This inertia can be an insidious problem, because the body is made up of physical substance, which is lethargic and inactive by nature. It can often require a direct injection of spiritual force to overcome this state of deliberate inactivity.

In a broader sense, the body's desire for ease and comfort often overrules and obscures the place of spirit in our life. The body loves its little indulgences—its comfort food, a soft bed, a massage, or perhaps a regular nap—and is likely to throw a tantrum if deprived of a special treat. There is nothing intrinsically wrong with a comfortable bed or a nap. But if these indulgences are given higher priority than serving spirit, they create an obstacle. The body ends up controlling us, rather than vice versa. It is a short step from this point to the attitude of wanting to avoid anything that might generate stress—like taking on new responsibilities. The "something extra" which is often the hallmark of spirit is seen as too risky.

Such people run a very real danger of cutting off all meaningful contact with spirit. It never occurs to them that the life of the body depends on the vitality of the soul. If our contact with the soul is strong, the likelihood is that our health will be good enough for whatever we need to do. To grow in our relationship to light, we must align all aspects of physical control with the design and intent of the higher self. We must teach the body to interact wisely and faithfully with the soul.

We must integrate the body with spirit.

But how do we integrate the physical body with something as ephemeral as a cloud? The key is to understand that we can, indeed, interact with clouds. When it rains, we generally let the inclement weather guide our plans for outdoor activities. If we have planned a picnic, for example, we will probably postpone it until a more suitable day. In this way, we let the weather control, or at least guide, our activities.

In the case of human consciousness, the cloud is our own spirit—the best within us. This spirit has a plan for our life, our activities, and our self-expression—a plan that is far more tailored to our needs and opportunities than the weather! All we need to do, in order to become responsive to this plan, is to invite it to guide and direct the physical body in specific, and the personality in general.

In short, we invite the best within us, our higher intelligence, to use its strength and wisdom to supervise and control the physical body. When we are tempted to overindulge the body's appetites, we ask the authority of spirit to overshadow us and strengthen our self-discipline.

When we are in danger of letting an illness overpower us and become the central absorbing issue of life, we invoke the healing power of spirit to mobilize our recuperative powers. When we are in danger of pushing spirit away, because we have let a handicap or limitation imprison our consciousness in form, we appeal to the awakening and revitalizing strength of spirit to help us regain our initiative. When we find we are spending too much time immersed in the pursuit of creature comforts, and not enough time acting as an agent of light, we need to call on the intent of spirit to reawaken us to our true work on earth.

It is the expectation of spirit that the personality will learn to do so. If the personality ignores opportunities to ask for this help, spirit will bypass its uncooperative personality—and exercise its control subconsciously or unconsciously. Perhaps the personality has harbored a resentment for thirty or forty years, carefully protecting it from the light of forgiveness of spirit. As the years unfold, this closely-held resentment becomes a cancer in the mind and the emotions. The soul warns the personality as often as it can to heed the consequences of holding onto this resentment, but the personality steadfastly—stubbornly—ignores all calls to change. Eventually, the higher self pushes the cancerous pattern of resentment into the dense physical body, where it begins to attack and devour physical cells. The objective of spirit is to awaken us to the need to overcome our resentment and heal this cancer, before it destroys us completely. Sometimes, however, the personality is so reluctant to cede control to spirit that the system ends up destroyed.

People who are focused in their physical bodies tend to misinterpret such messages. They blame the higher self for letting this cancer attack them, and shove spirit even further away. They wonder why spirit has abandoned them. Or they wonder why spirit is letting this cancer attack and kill the physical body. The true message, however, is vastly different. The cancer is a sign that we have clung to a destructive pattern too long—to a pattern that has estranged us from the life of spirit. We are not just dying—we are letting ourself become spiritually impoverished!

How must we respond to such messages? We need to regard them as invitations to impose a higher rhythm on our physical self-expression. We need to ask spirit to show us how we can use its forgiveness to purge our intolerance and resentment—and begin expressing compassion, not resentment, toward the problems of life. We need to ask spirit to show us how we can impose a higher rhythm on our daily life, so that we neutralize the devastating impact of our handicap or limitation. We need to give spirit the power to exercise its authority to keep the body from demanding excessive indulgences and favors that cause us to forget our need for spirit.

If we make these changes, we will find that the power of spirit to guide and control us is real and substantial—and has been trying to direct us in favorable ways, even though we have been ignoring it. We will also find that our capacity for pursuing the goals and fulfilling the duties of our daily life increases dramatically, in spite of ongoing hardships or illnesses.

Inspite of popular belief, old dogs can be taught new tricks. The physical body can learn to be guided and supported by spirit as well, no matter how ingrained old habits may be. The key lies in transforming our goals and habits in using the body, so that they conform to the design of the soul.

It is not necessary to force the body into rigid practices or customs. Spirit is not interested in punishing the body in any way, just controlling it. We gain nothing by trying to repress urges and appetites; in fact, if we try to repress them, our urges and appetites will well up in our imagination and become more difficult to manage.

The transformation that restores balance to the body must occur at the level of priority. The body is our primary tool for self-expression. It needs to be available, in good health, whenever spirit chooses to act. When spirit does not need it, the body may relax and renew itself in whatever ways it chooses—so long as it never becomes trapped in form.

The key factor is priority. If called on to serve the needs of spirit, does the body ignore the call because it needs a massage? Or because it must play a round of golf? Or because it is too tired to accept the challenge? If so, then the personality's priorities are askew. They have not been aligned to the design of spirit.

Some people, of course, make it very hard to change priorities, because they have installed certain regimens as the number one priority in their lives—even greater than spirit! They must therefore pursue their vegetarian diet, even if spirit is warning them that they are endangering their health. They must jog five miles every day, even if it distracts them from activities which could enrich human life.

At the extreme, such people "listen to what their body tells them," instead of making a similar effort to heed what the soul would tell them. The body has almost no wisdom or significance in and of itself. If it is not serving the design of the soul, its acts, beliefs, and priorities are almost without meaning. It is spirit that adds meaning and value to our existence—nothing else. It is therefore spirit that must be in control of how we treat and use the body.

The body is designed to do whatever the higher self instructs it to do. If we can transform our priorities and attitudes to enable this simple arrangement, we will have integrated the body with its spiritual design. If we do not, however, the body may anchor us in earthbound desires and frustrations.

As we demonstrate a capacity to heed the guidance of the soul, instead of listening to what our body tells us, a remarkable change occurs. With a spiritual agenda in control, the capacity and endurance of the physical body begins to increase. We find ourself better able to connect with patterns of health and vitality for others, as well as for ourself. Our rapport with the health and well-being of others increases.

We also discover a growing ability to attract to ourself a higher level of opportunity for spiritual service, as well as the people and resources we need to implement our plans. Our ability to be in the right place at the right time expands. Our capacity to make correct choices likewise matures.

Given enlightened spiritual supervision, the body will adapt to its ideal spiritual design. Its independence and resistance diminish as it becomes the servant of a loving master, the soul.

This is the secret of the centaur of mythology. The lower half may remain a horse, but it is under the perfect direction and control of the upper half, spirit. The two halves of the human being become one entity: an agent of light. Instead of being a body with a soul, as so many people would think, we recognize that we are spirit acting through form. The talents, skills, capacities, and potential of the physical body serve the needs and projects of the soul.

In order to practice this lesson of integrating the physical body with the design of spirit, we need to select an area in which we are excessively trapped in the whims of the body. It could be an area of addiction: eating, drinking, smoking, or drug taking. It could be a distorted need for sex or physical affection. Or it might be absorption in a health problem or a fitness regimen—perhaps even a handicap. It may be nothing more than the inertia of the physical form—or its constant demand to be pampered with indulgences.

Once we have chosen our target, we need to examine it. How do we interact with this condition? Do we succumb to it? Do we deny it? Do we punish the body for being weak? Do we rationalize our lack of responsiveness? Are we struggling to overcome this problem? How much energy have we invested in controlling the body—without success?

Next, we need to evaluate what the ideal resolution would be. Do we listen primarily to the body—and worry about it? Or are we trying to invoke the control and authority of spirit? What would be a practical level of balance in this aspect of life?

We must also evaluate what our priority in this regard ought to be. How can we realign our priorities to make them more responsive to the ideal plan of the soul, and less reactive to the demands and urges of the body?

How can we strengthen our endurance to cope with what we cannot immediately change?

Finally, we must consider what changes we need to make. Who is the boss in our life? Is it the body? Is it our own conscious awareness? Or is it the higher authority of the best within us, spirit?

What does it mean to invite spirit to take charge of the use of the body?

9.

Integrating Physical Events with Our Spiritual Destiny

In every aspect and event of life, there are two components: what we are and what we can become. As these dual forces interact with one another, they produce genuine growth in our aspiration, character, and behavior. But we sometimes miss the benefits of the marvelous interaction occurring in our life. We get caught up in the seeming disparity between the actual and the ideal, and become discouraged by life as it is rather than exalted by our insight into what our life is becoming! The resulting frustration can cause us great suffering and confusion—if we permit it. But no one ever needs to be trapped in this way by life. As Alexander Pope put it in his brilliant poem, *The Essay on Man*—

Submit—In this or any other sphere
Secure to be as blest as thou canst bear.

Instead of suffering, we can be as blessed as we can possibly imagine—and more so. But whether we are depends entirely upon us. Victims who choose to make a career out of suffering imprison themselves in unpleasantness. Those who choose to emphasize the ideal design of life, by contrast, achieve liberation.

The mystery of suffering lies in our ignorance of our power to become something greater than we are. Human suffering arises as we identify more with what is happening to us than with what we are meant to be. We trap ourself in our own dark imaginings, filled with visions of limitation and misery. We escape this prison in only one way: by discovering the ideal plan for greatness as created eons ago by spirit, and by recognizing how appropriately the current events and circumstances of our life enable us to enact this plan.

These twin elements—our plan for greatness and the events of our life—form what is commonly known as our "destiny." The concept of destiny is one that is poorly understood by most people—even most spiritual aspirants. Some people deny the existence of an intelligent plan in their life—which exposes them to the full brunt of suffering without any counterbalance to mitigate it. Other people fear or distort the idea of destiny; they look for it in terms of physical events, rather than sweeping patterns of growth and opportunity. Some are intimidated by the seeming multiplicity of events, worrying unnecessarily that they will be able to do "what they want" in the short span of years allotted to them. A few exceptionally blind people view the events of life as a kind of obstacle course. They believe that if they are able to dodge responsibility and charm their way to special indulgences, they will succeed. Unfortunately, these people generally remain clueless about the fact that they are succeeding only in cheating themselves of rich opportunities to grow.

The story of our destiny is the same for every man and woman. The personality loses confidence in the schemes and strategies that have earlier seemed to work; it begins to look for Plan B. Eventually, it learns that Plan B has been the ideal plan of spirit all along! By learning to respond to and cooperate with this Plan, we tap the full potency of human destiny—we become an agent of light. Pope described this achievement in some of the best lines of English poetry:

> God in the nature of each being founds
> Its proper bliss, and sets its proper bounds:
> But as he framed a Whole, the Whole to bless,
> On mutual Wants built mutual Happiness:
> So from the first, eternal Order ran,
> And creature linked to creature, man to man....
> God loves from Whole to Parts, but human soul
> Must rise from Individual to the Whole.

Our plan for expressing the light of the world, in other words, is part of a much larger plan—the plan of all humanity, which in turn is part of the plan of God. If we insist on miring ourself in our petty conflicts, we cannot participate consciously in the grand divine work.

By over-emphasizing our personal needs and wants, we mire ourself in a defensive posture toward life. But if we can rise from our personal focus to an appreciation of the Whole, we will stand on the threshold of liberation. We will begin to understand—and forgive—the seeming inconsistency of events and happenstance. We will also start to glimpse the patterns that give meaning to these events. Gradually, we will learn that when we actually do "submit" to the plan of our destiny, our awareness is flooded with the most sublime sense of rightness or justness. This is the presence of spirit rewarding correct behavior. As this awareness becomes stronger, we learn to access the Plan to guide and direct us in all that we do.

The work of discovering and activating this Plan within us is part of learning to embrace the light within us. In this instance, we learn to integrate the ordinary events of our personal daily life with the plan of destiny created for us long ago by the soul. As Pope put it:

Th' Eternal Art educing good from ill,
Grafts on this Passion our best principle;
'Tis thus the Mercury of Man is fixed,
Strong grows the Virtue with his nature mixed;
The dross cements what else were too refined,
And in one interest body acts with mind.

There are three common elements to activating our destiny, as determined by the divine design. These three elements are:

1. The need to learn and grow toward a common standard of maturity and spiritual wholeness.

2. The need to be useful to the larger Whole in which we live and move and have our being.

3. The need to become inclusive, recognizing that we share these common threads of purpose with all other people. We need therefore to stop thinking in tribal, narrowminded ways and begin identifying with universal values.

As our integration with spirit improves in these ways, we will discover within us a new capacity to act in life. Our competence will be enriched with a new measure of effectiveness. Our ability to face opposition will be refreshed with a touch of grace. And our capacity to take the challenges of life in stride will be uplifted by a pervasive sense of peace. In this way, we acquire the tools of spirit we need to transform the meaning of our experiences from threats and unpleasantries into opportunities for triumph and enlightenment.

We put the light to work.

This integration of the activities of our life with the soul's plan or destiny demands that we adopt a whole new approach to managing the duality of life. Some people are able to recognize well enough that old habits are no longer working for them, but they fail to take the next step and replace these old habits with new, more spiritual approaches. Instead, they try to hold onto the old habits by dressing them up in new clothes. Having been caught in lies and excuses, for example, they think that life is calling them to refine their manipulations and become even more deceitful than ever. It never occurs to them that their deceit is itself the core problem.

The work of integration always requires that we open ourself to and draw upon the magnificent resources of spirit. We must use these resources of spirit to replace old, disproven habits with new and better expressions of the light within us. Nothing less will do.

Highly competitive people who are forced by life's events to resign from positions of power in a cloud of disgrace, for example, must do more than renew their determination to win at all costs. They must replace it with a higher value of cooperating with ideals that serve the good of everyone concerned. They must come to understand that there is more to win in life through cooperation than there is through competition.

As we gain experience in bridging the gap between the duality of activity and destiny, we gain invaluable skill in linking heaven to earth. We break down the rigid concepts of personality that we have held for so long, and begin creating a new capacity for ongoing adaptability, constantly redefining who we are and what we can achieve.

Out of this effort, we slowly unfold—for all to see—new definitions of success, achievement, progress, usefulness, and the richness of life.

The human personality learns most rapidly by embracing an improper habit of conduct, defending it, and even prospering from it—and then having its impropriety dramatically exposed. As it reacts in disbelief to what it has done, the conscience of the personality resolves to find a better way.

It is therefore usually not enough just to define a higher virtue for living, based on divine law. This is just the first step in integrating this ideal into our self-expression. We must also learn to harness the power of this principle and apply it to our own habits of living, transforming them.

This transformation almost always involves a total reversal of our approach to life. If we have been defensive in dealing with competitive people at work, for example, it is foolish to think that the soul is going to bestow upon us a magical new power to embarrass and humiliate them! It will give us what we lack and need—greater patience, a capacity to forgive, and new skill in cooperating and achieving harmony.

None of this arrives instantly, however. We build these new habits and skills over a long period of time, as we deal with a wide variety of attempts to outsmart us, outvote us, and just plain oust us. If we can understand from the beginning, however, that we are building competence, while our competitive colleague is building only a debt to life, then we can see these episodes for what they are: lessons in the art of living.

It is therefore the better part of wisdom to assume that these lessons in living are helping us become a better person and encouraging us to fulfill our destiny. In fact, we should accelerate the process as much as we can, by reflecting on questions such as:

How can we become more useful in the work at hand?

How can we be more helpful to others serving the same inner goals as we?

How can we cooperate more intelligently—with others, with our creative self, and with the purpose of our work?

How can we transform conflict into harmony?

Where and how should we invest goodwill?

How can we become more mindful of the impact of our actions on others?

As we energize a new set of values in our thinking, they will begin to transform our character. It is therefore important to make a strong commitment to expressing these values in our daily activities. In this way, we work consciously to reduce the gap between our spiritual destiny and the mundane events of our life.

We become true to the light growing within us.

It is never enough, however, just to believe in spirit and let it pour through us. We must catch hold of its power and presence in our life and work it into our own fabric. We must therefore carefully examine the content of our subconscious and unconscious awareness, determining what existing structures of habit and association need to be changed by the emerging new values and principles of spirit.

It does us little good to align ourself with the spiritual force of patience, for example, it we continue to act with irritability and frustration in our daily life! We must instead become an agent for peace and learn to build conditions of serenity within our thoughts and emotions that will spill over into our activities, generating peace. We must give up our old reliance on fussiness and crustiness, and learn to approach challenging situations with quiet confidence and poise.

What in specific will we have to give up? Nothing important, really—just our habit of defensiveness, our denial of responsibility, our tendency to blame others for our own problems, our proclivity to expect others to make us happy, our victimhood, and all of our excuses and rationalizations. Even though this may seem overwhelming at first, when we at last gather all of these things together to get rid of them once and for all, we will find that they are almost nothing. Nothing at all.

If we are trying to become kinder and gentler, therefore, we must ask ourself: what old habits of mine will hinder this new direction? And what does it mean to correct them?

If we are trying to become more or less assertive, we must ask ourself: how do we tend to respond to or express authority? How are we apt to behave the next time our authority is challenged? How should we act?

In this manner, we create a mental template that lets us understand what changes in maturity are needed in order to make the required transformation. This template then lets us practice or rehearse ideal ways of acting before the need arises in our life. As a result, we will be far better prepared to act wisely when the occasion does arise.

Ideally, part of this template will include a means for monitoring our daily efforts to change. We will start examining daily events in terms of our new value. Is this an occasion for acting with greater patience? How will that help me? Will it enhance my growth and maturity as a person? Will it still serve me well as I become more loving and capable? Is this new approach to life truly helpful—or just self-serving?

A major key to transforming character is to see beyond our egotism and self-centeredness. Only then can we learn to respond to others with wisdom and goodwill. It is therefore important to evaluate our responses to life, asking: Is this how we want to be treated? Will this work for the good of everyone, not just us?

As we learn to interpret life through this template, we create a structure in consciousness capable of registering new insight from spirit. We learn, through our own experience, that we must rise from Individual to the Whole. We also learn the wisdom within another passage from *An Essay on Man*:

> Know then this truth (enough for Man to know)
> "Virtue alone is Happiness below."

The ideal design of life, translated by the enlightened mind first into divine virtues and then into noble values and beliefs, is the sole basis of contentment in the human being. It is also one of the first treasures of spirit that we receive as we learn to tread the spiritual path.

The full benefit of the work of integrating a grasp of our inner destiny with the events that play out in our life becomes obvious only when the work of integration is complete. Having learned to bridge the gap between the seeming duality of events and destiny, we cease analyzing events as good and bad. Instead of being threatened by opposition, we see it as an invitation to learn new skills and insights. Instead of being shocked by corruption in government—or the church—we see it as an opportunity for reform. The events are as much an opportunity to build as they are a threat or disaster. It is mostly a matter of how we choose to view them.

As we leave behind us our self-centered focus, which tries to convince us that everything is probably a threat, we begin to understand that wisdom always rules. Good intentions imposed without wisdom usually lead to utter catastrophe. The effort to be helpful can generate enormous harm, if we blunder about stupidly.

The same is true at global levels. Humanity needs to leave behind its tribalistic, narrowminded understanding of life, with its emphasis on ethnicity, class, and profession, its obsession with victimology. The attempt to preserve these traditions has trapped society as a whole every bit as much as self-centeredness traps the individual. But the key is the same as before: we must learn to embrace the Whole.

We are children of light. No event or humiliation can deprive us of this birthright, this eternal characteristic. When we forget this essential fact, we suffer. But as we grow in the wisdom of our own heritage, we cast off the shackles of suffering. We reclaim our destiny, our true spiritual heritage, and become, in full, an agent of light.

One of the best ways to put these ideas to work to help us grow is to examine an issue of life that consistently frustrates or irritates us.

1. How can we change ourself, as opposed to the situation? How can we enrich our habits or attitudes so that we begin to gain control of the impact of this issue on us?

2. What new skills do we need to cultivate—skills of coping; greater understanding; patience and forgiveness; courage and endurance; or perhaps cheerfulness and optimism?

3. What do we have to give up to make room for these new qualities and capacities?

Having assessed the transformation required, we must then create a vivid mental template in collaboration with spirit—a template which will invite spirit to supervise and inspire us as we strive to confront the situations of life with wisdom and love.

Our goal is to demonstrate that we can take charge of our life, if we connect it with spirit. We no longer need to be a victim, for we have discovered something much better. We have discovered the key to mastering the events of life.

10.

Integrating Conflict with Spiritual Growth

Each human life is punctuated by conflict. As young children, most of us were shielded from such turmoil; our parents loved and supported us and, if they quarreled with each other, they probably did it away from our view. But as we entered adulthood and began venturing into the world, we discovered that not everyone liked or adored us quite as much as our own family. We encounter people who disagree with our pet ideas; we find people who actively oppose us and our projects. Sometimes, we even invite conflict, by behaving inconsistently or immaturely.

There are several common ways people deal with conflict. One well-used ploy is to deny the problem: "I didn't do it." There is a fundamental flaw in this approach, however. If we did indeed do whatever it is we are denying, life will eventually expose us. At that point, not only must we deal with the original conflict, but also with the consequences of our rejection of accountability.

Another popular ploy is to avoid controversy by shifting responsibility to others. "I didn't do it—but he did." This act of blaming others usually backfires, though, because we have now broadened the conflict by making new enemies—the people we are accusing.

The most tempting of all common stratagems is intimidation. "I didn't do it—and I'll attack anyone who says I did." If someone challenges us, we strike back aggressively. As commonplace as this reaction is, it serves only to entrench the conflict.

The unpleasant truth is that denial, blame, and intimidation almost always deepen a conflict. These ploys escalate our involvement in the difficulty, instead of letting us manage it.

The enlightened alternative is to stop viewing conflict as a personal attack and begin recognizing the deeper meaning behind the conflict. Most conflicts arise only because we lack the spiritual qualities and skills that would have helped us avoid a bad situation, or at least diffuse the tension. This is a simple concept. We act impatiently because we lack patience. We speak bluntly and provoke others because we lack skills of effective communication. We criticize harshly because we lack understanding and kindness.

Obviously, if we cultivate the skills we need, then we can manage most or all situations without feeding conflict. Other people will still throw figurative stones at us, but we will be able to deflect them with our strength of character. The conflict quickly becomes one-sided, because we are able to take it in stride.

In fact, if we can understand the deeper meaning of the conflicts of our life, we can begin to see them as "wake up calls" from spirit—warnings to pay attention to our arrogance or dishonesty or self-centeredness. In many cases, it is also a warning that far greater conflicts lie ahead, if we fail to change. If we can learn the lessons behind events that irritate us, we will be immunized to handle major problems when they arise. But if we fail to learn now, the hope of handling future challenges dims.

The frustration that often accompanies conflict is also a message from spirit. Loosely translated, it is something like a "howler" telegram in a Harry Potter movie: "So, you thought you could handle life without paying attention to your inner spirit, eh? Well, look at you now. Frustrated, angry, and full of self-pity! That's not what I am looking for, you know! Why don't you try some maturity for a change! If you were willing to grow up, you wouldn't constantly be immersed in all of these conflicts!"

Of course, the idea that the soul is angry with the personality is an illusion. It is the personality, not the soul, that condemns itself once it understands the havoc it has set in motion unnecessarily. We must understand that the capacity of the soul to nurture growth is the precise faculty we need in order to handle conflict more maturely.

This should make perfect sense. Growth and conflict often reciprocate one another. Whenever we stop growing, conflict tends to arise. Conversely, conflict provides us with our best opportunities to grow. In either case, it is the perspective of the soul that enables us to grow in love and wisdom and neutralize conflict.

By integrating our capacity to grow with the conflicts we experience, we harness the power and qualities of the soul to help us manage turmoil. This lets us reduce our frustration and confusion.

We fear conflict only because our fear has not been neutralized by our capacity for endurance and self-control.

We despair in the midst of conflict only because we have not learned to think optimistically or act cheerfully.

We become angry only because we lack the goodwill and knowledge we need to face conflict with confidence and skill.

We retreat into apathy only because we lack the wisdom and strength to pursue solutions to the problems life has lain at our feet.

We think about giving up only because we have not fully called on our sense of personal honor and the support of our soul.

One habit that keeps us trapped in conflict is the tendency to misinterpret the true nature and origin of our conflict. The person or situation that annoys us is usually just the trigger for our own growth. Instead of focusing on this trigger and waiting for it to change or disappear, we must turn our eyes inward. We need to see that the conflicts of life are often the compelling stimuli that push us into making major advances in maturity and wisdom.

If we turn these "triggers" into enemies and demonize them, we make it virtually impossible to grow in any meaningful way from the conflict. We just energize our frustration and estrange ourself from the ideal solution of the soul—our need for greater patience, tolerance, skill, or understanding. We must therefore change our core definition of "conflict" and how we intend to deal with it. Only then can we embrace it fully.

This is seldom an easy lesson to master. The human personality has carefully constructed many habits of defensiveness that will block our better efforts. Often, the only way to gain control over these habits is to recognize how they keep us trapped in our problem—and how we desperately need something completely new and better—something that will actually work.

In other words, we must rise out of the fog of our pessimistic views and habits and recognize that the real world is not a sphere of difficulty. It is a place of abundance and opportunity, where maturity and cooperation are richly rewarded. When we extend respect to others, for example, they generally respond in kind. Those that do not are obviously still trapped in defensiveness. Instead of being angry with them, we should hold to the expectation that they will learn from our own good example.

This new attitude of optimism and respect makes it possible to begin reviewing constructive options for repairing the mess we have created, and defining practical ways to resolve the conflict. It is, in fact, the essential mind set for getting on the wavelength of growth.

The impulse to grow is alive and strong in each human being. It cannot be found, however, through endless psychological analysis of either our problems or our reactions to them. It is part of spirit. To tap it, therefore, we must rise above our conflicts and traumas and discover it in our interior essence.

Some people might wonder: if this impulse to grow is alive and strong within me, why have I not found it? The answer is simple. It is imprisoned by two types of destructive habits that we must reform. First, we need to disengage our carefully-tended defensive mechanisms. Second, we need to outgrow our habit of attacking the trigger instead of the real problem.

Far too often, we will not achieve this epiphany until we reach a level of defeat and exhaustion and cry out: "Is this all there is?" At that point, the soul answers, "No! Life is much greater and richer than what you have discovered on your own. Let me help you cultivate the eyes that can see this greater reality—the life of spirit."

If we are ready to listen, this moment can be a turning point in our life. God always meets us at our point of need—but we must take the first step, by taking our need and laying it, as a sacrifice, on the altar of the Lord, invoking His grace.

If we do so with an open heart, spirit will respond.

Once we have defined how we need to grow in order to repair the conflict we are immersed in, we need to discover what it means to act in a more mature way. We take stock of our conflicts. Instead of blaming our misery on either life or our enemies, we realize that they have been nothing but the vehicles for our growth! Needing an adversary to help us learn patience and tolerance, for instance, we have drawn to us someone willing to play that role. We must also realize that they will continue to play this role faithfully until we graduate from this assignment. In this way, we integrate our conflict into our agenda for growth.

This insight often occurs in an "eureka" kind of moment, as we discover that our true enemy is our own defensiveness. It is not life; life is designed to help us. It is not specific people; we have drawn them into our turmoil to compel our transformation. We should therefore be understanding, not bitter. Bitterness is a reaction that can trap us in conflict forever.

And so, if we want other people to trust us, we need to evaluate what changes we must make in order to win their support. Some people might regard this as repugnant, but they need to remember that the key to self-mastery is our own growth in maturity and character. No one achieves self-mastery by waiting for the world and everyone else in it to change. We achieve enlightenment through the growth we are willing to make unilaterally.

This growth must embrace a good deal more than the acceptance of a concept or a theory. We must develop a thorough plan of action for making the changes required to grow in these ways. A vague desire to be happy is not enough! We must decide what we are going to do in order to create fairness and happiness in our life, our relationships, and our duties.

In addition, we must remain vigilant, lest we succumb to the enormous pressure to slip back into old, defensive patterns of behavior. We must remember, on a regular basis, that we are seeking to integrate with the direction and agenda of spirit. We are seeking to implement its basic design for us. It is therefore important to resist backsliding.

One way of keeping our eyes focused on the goal is to realize that we will remain a victim of many conflicts for the rest of this life and probably several more, unless we break the chain of repetition now.

The choice is ours.

This work of self-mastery alters the way we view the conflicts of our lives. The events we used to regard as threats and opposition begin to be viewed as avenues to divine possibilities. We begin to see our experiences as part of a continuum of growth that we have been treading for a long, long time.

As long as we remain immersed in conflict, and view our life as filled with enemies and obstacles, we will suffer from mental myopia; that is, we will only be aware of the last step we have taken and the next one before us, and not have much of a clear view of them, either! We will continue to personalize and melodramatize our struggles, agonizing in pain and suffering.

As we learn to integrate these problems with our ability to grow, however, the spectrum of high possibilities begins to open up longer vistas. We can understand more of our past—and view the future more optimistically.

With this new degree of vision comes a new sense of responsibility. We come to understand that it is pointless to be overwhelmed by our sense of what is wrong; instead, we must concentrate our efforts on taking steps that will bear fruit in our life. The struggle to escape the pain of any conflict dooms us to relive the conflict perpetually, until we can manage it in more spiritual terms.

In order to harness our impulse to grow, in other words, we must be willing to embrace and accept conflict. We do not glorify it—but we do not runaway from it, either. Instead, we face it squarely—and focus our efforts on the spiritual vision within the problem.

In order to sustain this perspective, we must take steps to eliminate any attitudes that would otherwise perpetuate our sense of conflict. Some of the most notorious of these attitudes are:

Resentment—the habit of perpetuating our anger over some disappointment for the rest of our lifetime, often blaming life if not God for our unhappiness.

Hopelessness—the state of feeling that we have been battered so extensively that we cannot even imagine any improvement. We are doomed to suffer.

Cynicism—the notion that life is designed to punish us for unknown sins, or for no reason at all. We curse the misfortune of our birth.

Alienation—the indignities we have been forced to endure are so great that we have become completely estranged from any sense of goodness or purpose.

The presence of any of these attitudes in our interaction with life repels the life of spirit. In order to become an agent of light, therefore, we must seek to eliminate them from our character. This may require us to move out of our comfort zone and challenge the obsessions that entrap us.

We must replace our resentment about what is wrong with sincere thankfulness for the blessings we have.

We must replace hopelessness about what we lack with a mature respect for our own accomplishments and inner strength.

We must replace cynicism toward our disappointments with a mature regard for divine and human potential.

We must replace alienation from life with gratitude for the support of our friends and spirit—in particular, its loving design for our life.

As we learn to transform the conflicts of life into opportunities for spiritual growth, we discover new seeds of talent and maturity within the fertile ground of our own lifetime. In fact, we will find that we have created a whole new vision about the meaning of our life!

This vision helps us understand that the conflicts of life are designed to be stepping stones to wholeness. They are not handicaps causing us unlimited stress; instead, they are a provocation prodding us to search out and find new and better ways to confront life—ways based on the qualities of spirit, rather than the immaturity and defensiveness of the personality.

In this expanded awareness of the benevolence of life, we begin to recognize the futility of being angry about injustice or sad about our losses; the pointlessness of being frightened by danger or pessimistic about the future of humanity. After all, if spirit has planned a noble future for humanity, which it has, isn't our own closely-held pessimism an utter waste of time and effort? Isn't it a rather pitiful attempt to protect us from bogey men that we should have outgrown when we were six?

Immature reactions to the struggles of life restrict our humanity and entrap us in the marsh of material-ism. Learning to integrate conflict with our capacity to grow liberates us from the dark recesses of life on earth. This liberation in turn produces a new level of empowerment; instead of quailing before the prospect of conflict and opposition, we see them as bridges to heaven—bridges we build with our own human skill and maturity.

We also get new insight into what the Christ was saying in the Beatitudes: "Blessed are the peacemakers, because they shall be called the sons of God."

By making peace with life, we become an agent of light.

The work to integrate conflict with the impulse to grow begins with the question: what is our weakest link? More than anything else, what draws to us conflict and turmoil? The answer will be some immature habit of personal defensiveness, be it aggressiveness, arrogance, stubbornness, or selfishness.

We must then inquire: how much of the richness of life have we missed by failing to correct this problem? How much of the kingdom of heaven are we willing to forego in order to preserve other habits? How much of the burden of earth are we willing to bear before we choose liberation?

Next, we should take inventory: how much progress have we already made in this lifetime in overcoming this problem? Where have we taught ourself to cultivate a positive outlook, instead of the gloom and doom we experienced earlier? How can we build on this progress? How can we attract the loving support of spirit in this effort?

It is also important to define precisely how we sabotage our better efforts. What subconscious patterns reinforce our slavery to suffering and turmoil? How can we regain control of our emotions?

This prepares us for the centerpiece of the work: how can we reach out to spirit for greater support? How can we become more continually mindful of its presence and guidance in our life? How can we infuse more of its love and joy into our own attitudes, to exalt us and strengthen us to seize control of the citadel?

Above all, we must consciously cultivate the vision that our struggle in life, whatever it is, is indeed worthwhile. We are building a connection with inner peace that will release us permanently from the shackles of suffering. In this way, we embrace a new vision of heaven as well.

We understand, along with Alexander Pope, it is part of our work on earth to rise above conflict and find the unifying wholeness of human life:

Condition, circumstance is not the thing;
Bliss is the same in subject or in king,
In who obtain defense, or who defend,
In him who is, or him who finds a friend;
Heaven breathes through every member of the whole
One common blessing, as one common soul.

11.

Integrating Opportunities to Act with Cycles of Time

In this era of democracy, it is popular to champion our individuality. But as we tread the spiritual path, we must also remember the teachings of the ancient wisdom: that each of us is a microcosm within a macrocosm—a small spark of light within a giant sphere of illumination. There is much this tiny spark of light can learn to do, but we must never forget that it exists within the context of the laws and nature of divine life.

For this reason, our capacity to act individually is often limited and even shaped by forces and factors beyond our personal control. People who are still immersed in discovering the nature of individuality often resent this idea—and thereby fail to comprehend it. But as we explore the nature of individuality, we begin to find that it is not the answer to all problems. We learn that the human personality is finite and focused. Life goes on, even if the physical body ails. Wisdom and love continue, even if we behave foolishly or selfishly. Divine law continues to operate, even if we ignore or abuse it.

Spurred by these discoveries, we start to explore the larger realms of life. But even then, we may well ignore the implications of this larger life on our personal affairs. We are still too absorbed in the needs and pains of the personality. We might be seized, for example, with the idea of helping needy people. But if we abandon our own responsibilities to family and work in order to help others, we are probably not acting wisely. We are making a potentially noble sacrifice at the wrong time in our life, thereby nullifying its nobility.

In the West in particular, we need to understand that there is a right time to act as well as a right way. Many people have an excellent grasp of what needs to be done, but act on it impulsively, before conditions are ripe. A common example would be a fellow with a family to support who quits his job impulsively, without lining up another.

Acting out of harmony with right timing is a cultural problem as well as a personal one. The West does not prize patience and timing as virtues. Business people, for example, value efficiency, cost-cutting, and "getting it done now," instead of working with the ebb and flow of economic tides. Politicians tend to view all major issues as "crises" and demand immediate reform, without researching all of the likely consequences. The telling example of this impetuosity was the Great Society, an ambitious political plan that declared war on poverty—and lost. Billions of dollars have been spent over the last thirty years without any noticeable improvement.

Another common example of acting out of tune with time is the perfectionist who insists on being fully prepared before taking any action in life. As a result, he waits too long to act, or never acts at all. He lets ideal windows of opportunity slip by without taking advantage of them.

Oddly, people with massive inferiority complexes often act in exactly the same way—and for much the same reason. They "know" they are not ready to act, so they refuse to utilize the talents and resources they have. They retreat from life, rather than risk failure or further loss of confidence.

We live in an ever-changing world. The structure of life may or may not change appreciably, but the tides of opportunity are constantly sweeping through society. If we are attempting to live purposefully and constructively within this society, we need to pay attention to these invisible tides. Like a golfer checking wind direction, we need constantly to check if the winds of time are with us—or against us.

The ability to act with right timing is an intuitive skill we are all designed to develop. It is a tremendous asset in our capacity to approach life creatively—and to serve as an agent of light. Just as there are times when the economy is strong and other times when it is weak, there are times in human affairs that favor innovation and risk—and other times which call for caution and patience.

This intuitive skill is developed by integrating our acts and activities with the inner patterns and laws that are meant to guide them. It is easy enough to observe these patterns—after the fact. But if we take the next step, and integrate our intuitive sense of timing with our acts, we will be able to align our decisions and projects with the ideal moment in time. We will be able to seize opportunity and put it to work in our life.

The ability to work in this way with the principle of right timing liberates us from fate and random chance. We not only learn to recognize the emerging patterns of life before they arise, but also discover how our creative efforts can lead to innovation and reform.

Whether we are dealing with individual or cultural movements, new impulses emerge into manifestation in the physical world in recognizeable patterns. In order to refine our intuitive sense of right timing, we need to learn to perceive these patterns—in our activities, in our nation, and in the world—and listen to the messages they convey.

The pattern of timing for any event, large or small, consists of four stages. These four stages are:

1. Incubation. We grow aware that something is brewing at deep unconscious levels. If we are already somewhat intuitive, we may become aware of new forces and pressures coming our way—or even become alert to a new nexus of interconnecting possibilities, forming opportunity. If we are not especially intuitive, we will probably begin to sense a growing uneasiness or discon-

tent with some aspect of life—the very aspect which is ripe for change. We look for new answers.

2. Innovation. We start to be tantalized by the prospect of initiating something new. Our discontent may grow into a sharp dissatisfaction with conditions at work or in a relationship. We form a resolve to reform these conditions, or perhaps try something new.

3. Change. The mounting tide of change forces the issue into the open. It is no longer possible to ignore the problem; the status quo must be amended or corrected. If we seek to deny the problem at this point, we will miss a wonderful opportunity for progress; conversely, if we are ready to act, we can make giant leaps forward.

4. Consolidation. Every step forward encounters resistance from the old, established ways until a "new normal" arises. In this final stage, priorities must be redefined, cycles reinterpreted, and methods modified. The period of consolidation completes the process of change, cementing the new pattern as a habit or a tradition.

Every major phase of our personal life will be at differing stages of the timing process. Our parents may be approaching death, our children may just be discovering the importance of values, our marriage may be maturing into new levels, and our relationship with spirit may be on the verge of a new breakthrough. Each kind of experience presents its own distinct opportunity. We need to define what this opportunity is—and act accordingly.

The same idea applies to world events. A strong international tide has been enriching the abundance of the world during the past one hundred years. But some countries are just now discovering the need to participate actively in this process. Others are confronting an atavistic retreat into fundamentalism, while still other countries are absorbed in preening their all-consuming selfishness. The more advanced societies face the opportunity to share their culture and skill with others—sometimes willingly, sometimes reluctantly.

In order to work with the principle of right timing, we must be able to see the opportunity within each of the four phases of change.

The opportunity of incubation requires us to be open to new ideas. It is a time for patience and discovery—a time to hold a positive expectancy that the conditions of life are evolving, even if we cannot quite define how.

The opportunity of innovation requires us to explore, experiment, and discover. We need to be flexible and willing to take risks, until we can see what works and what does not. It is a time for restraining stubbornness and judgmentalism.

The opportunity of change requires optimism and confidence. This is the time to act on new plans, and we need a strong confidence in our ability to make these changes successfully. It is too late to entertain doubts that should have been overcome during the incubation phase.

The opportunity of consolidation requires us to review the progress we have made. What have we learned? Where have we failed to reach our goal? How should we revise or reform our priorities and efforts? What values do we need to strengthen and glorify, so that we will be ready for the next cycle—which is about to begin!

Having made this assessment of an activity, we can then use the same matrix to determine how we can best capitalize on the situation at hand.

If the situation is still in the incubation phase, we entertain various possibilities. Is this pattern a repetition of earlier cycles in our life? Did we handle those opportunities wisely, or did we squander them? Did we make mistakes we ought to avoid—or did we act in ways that bear repeating? What new directions is spirit trying to impress upon us? Incubation is a time for patient observation; a time when we try to register incoming force.

The phenomenon of mid-life crisis is a good example of how this period of incubation ought to work. Many people in their mid-thirties begin to experience a sense of uneasiness about what they have accomplished, what they have neglected, and where they are heading. They review assumptions and goals made as a teen or young adult. In truth, they are responding (without knowing it) to a new and stronger investment of spirit in their lives. In many people, this contact awakens very little except a guilty conscience. In others, it stirs up a vague sense that there is more to life than they have discovered so far. If these people let their immaturity guide them as they respond to the new impulses, they will probably make decisions they eventually rue. But if they view this as a healthy time of incubation, and focus their attention more specifically on new spiritual direction, they can harness the opportunities of this time.

If conditions have moved into the innovative phase,

we need to give ourself permission to experiment with different alternatives. Perhaps a sales person has found that sales have been dropping. He still believes in his product, but needs to find new ways to present it to his customers. He needs to ask himself: how can I refocus my efforts? What would be truly innovative? How will I know it? What should I avoid? As he seeks out these answers, his focus will draw to him the help and contacts he needs.

If we find ourself in the heart of change, we need to respond with competence, enthusiasm, and a strong willingness to reform as needed. Here is an opportunity to improve our efficiency, let go of worn-out beliefs, and revise our thinking. We cannot afford to let it slip by.

A good example of seizing this kind of opportunity would be a marriage that is in transition. The couple is outgrowing the honeymoon stage of being desperately in love with one another. They are confronting the challenges of raising kids, paying bills, and establishing themselves in their community. If they seize the oppor-tunity of the time wisely, they will come closer together and discover a new plateau of love and respect that far transcends the giddiness of "being in love." It is defi-nitely not a time to doubt the value of the marriage.

Once we move into the phase of consolidation, the focus of our efforts should be to celebrate and maximize the rewards of whatever change has occurred. We need to look back onto the whole process of change, and see what benefits we have accrued. What new strengths and maturity have we acquired, in spite of any hardship? How can we continue to benefit from the effort we have made?

A good example of this phase of consolidation would be the person in his thirties who looks back and sees that he did not benefit as much as he could have from his college education. He therefore seeks advice from mentors, takes new training, and studiously researches journals and books. In this way, he may be unconsciously preparing himself for a promotion at work—or the opportunity to inspire his own children with a love of education that he did not discover until halfway through his life.

One aspect of divine grace is that no opportunity is ever completely wasted. We may fail to act at the optimum moment, but the impulse to grow keeps circling back, inviting us to pay attention to whatever we have ignored.

The major impediment to this sense of right timing is smallmindedness—an amalgam of arrogance and ignorance. We trap ourself in the trivial aspects of the current moment, and fail to look at the larger context in which this moment is occurring. We ignore the plan of spirit for our life, thinking only of this moment's measure of stress or happiness. As a result, we act impatiently, rashly, and aggressively. We believe we know all of the answers, when in fact we know almost nothing.

In order to overcome this smallmindedness, we must transform our pettiness. We must become more inclusive, cultivating a sense of continuity in the purpose and consequences of our choices. We need to be able to look to the future as well as past experiences, stretching our imaginations at both ends of the spectrum. We also need to cultivate a larger perspective that embraces the purposes of spirit.

We must give up our desire for simplistic solutions, and begin to develop a deeper respect for the delicacy and complexity of life, as well as a respect for the spiritual laws of life. In particular, we must learn about the law of cause and effect, and begin to understand how it has worked out in our own life. We must comprehend that immature acts tend to produce unpleasant consequences.

Another key to demolishing smallmindedness is to transform our tendency of self-absorption by generating respect for the needs of others. Different people have different needs and temperaments. We must resist the temptation to force others to conform to our own expectations and methods. We must cultivate tolerance.

Ultimately, this effort leads us to learn to respond to spiritual guidance, both consciously and unconsciously. We must forego the temptation to react to life selfishly; we must forge an active partnership with the soul.

As we integrate with the purposes and guidance of the soul, we begin to think in new ways. We develop an inner sense of equilibrium that reinforces the right decisions we make. The rational mind may quickly become exhausted trying to interpret this guidance, but no matter: our intuitive skills will soon take its place. Step by step, we will learn to be guided by the cycles and plans of the soul.

Through this conscious effort to grow, we develop a strong awareness of the inner rhythms of life. There are many such rhythms, but the most important in this regard are the rhythms of creation, innovation, reform, and fulfillment—the rhythms of growth and change.

Slowly, we move away from linear thinking, entering the previously uncharted seas of multidimensional thinking. We become an agent of time as well as light, much better prepared to act wisely within the complex fabric of life. We become familiar within the inner structure of life—including the inner structure of time. We can scan the plan of the soul for our life, and see it within the context of divine law and spiritual intention.

At this point, we realize that change occurs in form only as we incorporate into our self-expression the timeless, immortal qualities of spirit. What is important, therefore, is not change, but the maturity, skill, and wisdom that accompany it. Time is not a limitation to our self-expression; it is a creative medium for our growth.

In fact, our perception of time is largely an illusion created by our emotional expectations and our mental perceptions. The more we integrate our opportunities with spiritual patterns and divine cycles of life, the more we penetrate this illusion and see clearly. We know, in the words of St. Teresa: "With patience, all things can be achieved."

The best exercise we can pursue to integrate the activities of life with opportunities for growth is to review our relationship with spirit.

What is incubating? What is brewing in unconscious levels of our life? How are we dissatisfied with present conditions?

What is on the verge of change? What new lines of thought and self-expression are emerging in our life? What is sabotaging it? Where are we stuck in old habits and expectations? What keeps us stuck—our apathy, fear, or limited imagination? What new ideas pop into our awareness?

What is ready to appear? What is the opportunity for growth the soul has laid at our feet? How can we capitalize on this? How are we letting doubt hold us back?

What needs to be consolidated? What lessons have we learned in our years of spiritual growth? How can we build on them? How should we update our agenda and motives? Have we collected—and celebrated—the full reward of the effort we have made?

12.

Integrating Patterns from the Past with Spiritual Potential

As we achieve greater contact with spirit, we unlock the door to new awareness, greater creative potential, and expanded opportunities to serve. But this development can bring with it a whole new level of frustration, because we may find that our life circumstances do not measure up to our new standards and our desire to be useful. We may feel limited by our marriage, cramped by an uninspiring job, cheated by the lack of a proper education, or confined by a crippling illness. We wonder why life thwarts us in these ways—just at the moment when we are ready to serve!

In the second installment of the Harry Potter story, Professor Dumbledore tells Harry: "It is our choices, Harry, that show what we truly are, far more than our abilities." He was explaining why Harry shared so many talents with Voldemort, yet took a completely different path. Harry was no more "special" than Voldemort—but he had made more enlightened choices.

This is a lesson all agents of light must learn. No one is ever thwarted by life; the obstacles we stumble over are the consequences of choices we have made in the past. These choices were reactions of fear or greed or sadness or anger or selfishness. As we discover and attune to the life of spirit, we outgrow—perhaps even repudiate—these choices. But we may not completely disengage them. Unless we take specific action, they will remain as patterns in our subsconscious—patterns that will continue to lead us into the shadows and swamps of life. As such, they usurp the authority of the soul to guide us benevolently. Unawares, we continue to trip over our own selves!

Our problem is a simple one. In our zeal to strengthen our contact with the soul, we tend to overlook or even discount the more pedestrian assignment of mental housecleaning—the process of realigning our habits, attitudes, beliefs, and motives so that they are vitalized by spirit, not energized by fear, hatred, jealousy, cruelty, or greed. In other words, we ignore the work of integration—specifically the integration of automatic patterns from our past into the wisdom, love, and authority of the soul.

As we approach the life of spirit, for example, we may cling to massive amounts of anger. It is not possible to work with real spiritual force, however, as long as we remain trapped in an unwillingness to forgive. We must learn to focus the goodwill of spirit into our awareness to dispel and destroy lingering patterns of anger and hate.

Likewise, we often retain habits of self-centeredness and defensiveness long after we embark on the spiritual path. We remain absorbed in attending to our private concerns, instead of refocusing our attention on the higher, more loving perspective of the soul. What guidance and love does seep in from the soul is quickly reconfigured to support our own selfish interests. We miss almost all of the real spiritual component.

Self-pity is another common example. Instead of adopting the effortless, easy gracefulness of spirit, we cling desperately to the notion that life is a struggle and no one suffers more than we. What we fail to recognize is that suffering magnifies our entrapment in form; it eclipses the light of spirit that could otherwise assist us.

In each of these instances, we are using the established patterns of our past to obstruct our current spiritual growth. We may meditate or pray diligently every day, and yet we make little or no progress. Why? Because we make the fundamental mistake of expecting spirit to change "the life out there" instead of "the life within us."

Most people project their problems on others and the world around them: *the life out there.* Shortcomings are blamed on others; failures are blamed on circumstance or society. As a result, they succcumb to the glamour that life is unfair. In fact, however, life is exquisitely fair.

We attract circumstances, friends, and opportunities that reflect the content of our own character and behavior. When our character is marred by rationalization, guilt, and malice, we draw to us events that will reinforce our callow view. Any real contact with spirit becomes next to impossible.

If we are going to master the art of living, we must grasp the role of the life within us in directing everything we do. Ideally, our habits, beliefs, values, and character are linked directly to the light of spirit. But this linkage does not occur automatically, by believing in God. It develops as we build it—by integrating the light of spirit into our character.

The failure to integrate spirit into our character keeps us earthbound, even if we profess a great love for spirit. If this is so, we may have learned the words, but we are still not singing the hymn! We deny ourself the real power of spirit—the soul's ability to lead us wisely and seize upon genuine opportunity.

It is therefore of great importance to learn to use the skill of integration to focus the light of spirit into the patterns of our past, updating them so that we start being guided by spirit instead of leftover habits of vanity and venality.

The proper integration of spirit with the patterns of our past begins by conducting a thorough examination of our attitudes, beliefs, habits, motive, expectations, style, sense of purpose, and sense of identity. Much of what we discover will be patterns that work quite well for us.

A trait of optimism, for example, is easily aligned with spirit, as it already reflects the essence of inner poise. Such patterns of maturity need only be enriched by spirit, rather than modified.

But there will also be patterns that require a major overhaul in order to make them ready to be responsive to spirit. An ingrained habit of pessimism and defeatism, for example, directly contradicts the designs of spirit. So it would have to be thoroughly disengaged from all of our thoughts and beliefs, values and goals, before we could begin establishing more proper patterns.

In such a case, we need to appreciate that our contacts with spirit have given us a new lens through which we can view life. Instead of regarding anger as a necesssary tool of self-defense, we begin to see the damage it has caused and the havoc it has wreaked in our life. The lens of the soul lets enough light shine into our activities that we start to register new alternatives, new possibilities. In this way, we begin to understand the need for new methods in dealing with the imperfections and threats of life—methods based on the compassion and goodwill of spirit, rather than the self-centeredness of the personality.

The great majority of people identify with their moods, habits, and experiences—rather than the life of spirit. As a result, they carelessly fall into the belief that they are a "victim," if they have been abused; that they must be an antagonist, because they have encountered hostility; or that they have a right to be defeatist, because they have been disappointed. Such people are actually well-integrated—not with spiritual virtues, but with the false idols of ego, selfishness, righteousness, and defensiveness. They have boxed themselves into a rigid perspective that gives them almost no hope for relief.

In order to restore hope, these people need to learn to cultivate the perspective of spirit toward their lives. They need to see that they have closed down opportunities through their pessimism; that they have shut off avenues of help by identifying themselves as victims. They have made poor choices, and have cultivated a lifestyle that repeats those bad choices over and over, until they learn to break the repetitive pattern.

This dilemma is very much like listening to the evening news and tiring of all the negativity. If we are connected with spirit, the soul will help us remember to look for the good that is unfolding behind the horrific headlines. It is not a wise choice to turn the channel and watch reruns of *Happy Days* instead!

We must therefore understand that having a sickly body does not define who we are. Being a liberal or a conservative does not define who we are. Being betrayed by a friend does not define who we are. No event in life can ever define who we are, because our sense of identity derives from spirit.

As part of this examination of mental housecleaning, we must also review our current possibilities and potential. Are we judging life from a spiritual perspective—or do we pass judgments in less intelligent ways:

• By planning how we can defeat our enemies.
• By making decisions based on achieving greatest comfort at minimum risk?

• By wondering how we can extricate ourself from an embarrassing situation without further humiliation?

• By plotting how we can evade our duties.

• By devising schemes for blaming others for our failings.

• By inventing ways to feel good about ourself spiritually even though we are ignoring the soul.

The flaw in each of these options is that it makes us somehow dependent on "the life out there." None of these options actually helps us cultivate "the life within us."

The life of spirit is very much interested in working cooperatively with genuine efforts to harness our current potential more completely. To tap this power, however, we must start asking questions such as:

• How can we expand and improve our current use of our strengths and talents?

• Where do we need to become more loving and forgiving?

• When would it help us to become more cheerful and optimistic?

• Why are we waiting for something "out there" to happen? We need to take charge of our life and act!

The answers to this kind of questioning are not likely to be earth-shattering—but they will be profound. They will enable us to see how we can contribute to life even though we are not wealthy; how we can cultivate wisdom even though we might not have gone to college; how we can forgive others even though they may be unable to forgive us; and how we can greet unpleasant events in life with dignity and detachment.

The plain truth is that we do not need special circumstances in order to be heroic, helpful, considerate, wise, or noble. These virtues are within the grasp of every human being—especially every spiritual aspirant. So, even if we truly believe that we have no talents or opportunities, we do. Every day brings dozens of opportunities to act with more grace, greater insight, and renewed vitality.

In short, we do not have to wait for the world out there to change to suit us. We have the power and duty to make intelligent choices in our life. We need to see that there are always alternative ways to act in every situation.

We just need to learn to choose the alternative that best serves the life of spirit.

As we review the patterns of our past in this way, we will discover that the soul has had a plan for our life from the very beginning. We may have been unaware of it, or failed to appreciate it, but now we have the opportunity to activate it more consciously. It is as though the soul is inviting us to harvest the wisdom with which it first created this plan! By tapping this wisdom and learning to comprehend the benevolence in everything that has happened to us, we broaden our capacity to look at life as the soul views it.

We also tap the power to revise our character so that it better expresses the wisdom and love of the soul. Instead of viewing a defeat as proof of our incompetence, we see that in fact it was a vital experience in learning to become a stronger and more talented person. Instead of viewing a disaster as a personal insult or punishment, we see it as an opportunity to grow in maturity. Instead of viewing an illness or accident as an outrage, we see it as a helpful event that led us to better understand healing. Instead of viewing dysfunctional parents as a liability, we embrace them with gratitude—thankful that they helped us see the destructiveness of their behavior and the need for greater discipline and maturity in our own character.

Without the ability to choose wisely, Harry would have ended up a clone of Voldemort. Just so, if we fail to combine our examination of past trends with a new ability to choose wisely, our character will stagnate. We will be trapped in our own limitations—a slave to petty annoyance rather than a liberated agent of light.

We must understand that we are not just adopting new moods and opinions about life. We are harnessing the power of spirit to reform and upgrade our most fundamental values, ethics, habits, attitudes, and beliefs—including our sense of identity and worth. Our goal is to produce effective, long-term changes in our approach to life. We are striving to produce meaningful integration, not just relief from our distress.

For this reason, we should focus on one facet of life at a time, devoting at least several months to working on it. Having decided, for example, to stop being pessimistic, we must work on this challenge exclusively until we have registered substantial progress.

First, we must define what an enlightened solution to this problem is. In the case of pessimism, we must obviously learn to be optimistic and cheerful. But what does it mean to be realistically optimistic? We cannot just swing to the opposite extreme and become utopian and naïvely hopeful! We still face the same obstacles and hardships that challenged us when we were a pessimist. But now we realize that our pessimism was a reaction to life out there; it was not a choice of our inner life. Having decided to make intelligent choices from now on, we are quite correct in viewing every problem as an adventure in becoming enlightened. And that is cause for optimism!

Once we have defined optimism correctly, our next step is to consider how we are interfering with its natural development. If left to itself, the soul would flood the personality with pure optimism and joy. Since we have been pessismistic and cynical until now, something must have interfered with our natural expression of optimism.

This "something" is not so much the "tragedies" of life as it is the grim and skeptical attitudes entrenched in our subconscious. Somehow, we have cultivated a knee-jerk reaction of negativity and doom to life's events. How did this attitude develop? How do we perpetuate it? How are we starving ourself of divine joy and optimism?

The third step is to examine where we have developed a capacity to be optimistic in spite of this entrenched habit. No one is one hundred percent pessimistic. We may find, for example, that we are optimistic about the future of our children, even though we are all gloom and doom in other aspects of life. If we can transfer some of the optimism we experience in our family circle to the rest of our life, we can revise our subconscious more rapidly. We will also realize that we have been responsive to the guidance of the soul at least some of the time—which gives us a great boost in our efforts to become responsive all of the time.

The final step is to reflect on why it is important to make these changes. We realize, for example, that every change we make frees us from the pitfalls of the past—and brings us closer to our spiritual self. Simply put, life becomes more enjoyable whenever we are better able to express our spiritual design—as opposed to having constantly to clean up problem after problem caused by petulance, suspicion, and inertia.

As we integrate the patterns of our past with the opportunities of the present in this way, we learn a practical lesson in harnessing the light of spirit. Fresh light begins to emerge in our inner life—and in our outer life as well. We still have problems to face and losses to endure, but we are able to face them with a new ally: our inner spirit.

Clearly, we will not master this technique of integration unlesss we employ it in our life. We should therefore select a habit of importance—stubbornness, defensiveness, anger, or whatever—and work on revising it.

Our first step is to define clearly an enlightened alternative to the way we have been acting. As much as possible, we should try to define it as the soul views it.

Once we have defined the enlightened alternative, we need to examine how we are interfering with its expression. If we lack patience, for example, then what habits and beliefs eclipse the light of the soul that would otherwise flood us with patience? How did we build up these habits? What will it mean to "unlearn" them?

The third step is to take stock of times and situations when we have been able to act with patience. Is it possible to transfer the essence of the patience we have expressed at those times into the rest of our character?

Finally, we must reflect on why it is important to make these changes. We are not just becoming a better human being; we are investing in the life of our soul. We are enriching our mind and character with the treasures of spirit. We are turning out the old to make way for the new.

We are, in short, learning to make enlightened choices about life.

13.

Integrating the Personality with the Soul

A fundamental question every one of us seeking to become an agent of light must ask—and answer—is: how much of the life of spirit do we need in order to live a full life as a spiritual person? Is an occasional glimpse of inner reality enough? Or must we strive for a steady, unbroken contact flowing through every facet of our life?

The temptation to the spiritual novice (and more than a few who are no longer novices) is to try to trivialize the process of becoming spiritual. Instead of rushing to embrace the life of spirit in its fullest measure—to drink deeply of inner wisdom, love, will, and joy—many people try to lower the relevance of spirit to meet their personal requirements:

• They try to substitute avid religious rituals for genuine spiritual integration.

• They try to replace legitimate spiritual maturity with an inflated self-esteem.

• They define an occasional peek into the mind of God as an important "peak" experience.

• They try to practice spiritual centeredness by cultivating an uncaring and indifferent perspective on life.

• They regard conspicuous suffering—which they are usually good at—as a sign of true spirituality.

One of the most common problems made by people who are not fully integrated with spirit is the tendency to stop too soon. They learn to express peace and joy within their family circle and professional environment, yet never test themselves to see if they can express these divine qualities in more demanding circumstances. As a result, they tend to over-estimate their true level of maturity.

In this vein, some people will develop excellent habits of patience or goodwill, and then assume that their work on the spiritual path is complete—forgetting that the divine life expresses wisdom, joy, harmony, beauty, dignity, strength, and creativity as well as serenity and love. The mastery of one or two spiritual virtues is a good starting point—but just the first step on a long path. Eventually, we are called to master all spiritual qualities, not just the ones that appeal to us.

Many Christians, for example, believe that a strong, unwavering faith in God is all that they need; they may even assume that the effort to cultivate other spiritual skills would somehow weaken their faith. Such people are unquestionably sincere, but they remain largely empty in a spiritual sense. They have deliberately impoverished themselves instead of accepting the rich abundance of the inner life.

The primary duty of agents of light is to integrate the life of spirit into the personality and their behavior, so that heaven comes to earth in human form. This effort progresses step by step, lesson by lesson. It does not conclude until we have learned to "download" every possible spiritual force available to the human race and have translated these qualities into dynamic expressions of spiritual maturity, grounded in our daily activities and character. It is not enough to be inspired by these forces at abstract levels. In addition to loving peace, we must become a peacemaker in our own life. In addition to being inspired by creative ideas, we must apply these ideas creatively to improve human life.

The work of integration calls us to learn to harness wave after wave of refinement in three key areas of spiritual development:

1. Investigation.
2. Introspection.
3. Investiture.

This challenge is not something that can be met in a few meditations scattered here and there. It is not met in full until the spiritual will becomes our purpose and direction, spiritual wisdom illumines our understanding of life, and spiritual love governs the heart of our self-expression.

The first major arena of spiritual integration is **inves-**

tigation. We must learn the basic intuitive skills of sailing forth into the abstract mind and discovering the unseen design of God.

Some people believe that this direct exploration of the mind of God is unnecessary; all that they need to know, they think, is contained in scripture. The scriptures of all major religions are invaluable aids to our effort, of course, but they are meant to serve as comprehensive road maps—not as substitutes for spiritual experience! There is a difference between reading a map that shows the route to Cancun, and actually traveling to and spending a week there! Scripture can set us on the right track, but we still must make the journey of discovery for ourself.

It is not just scripture that reveals the inner design and laws of God. All of creation does. A tiny flower, a bear in hibernation, the structure of a molecule, or the appearance of a new star in the night sky can lead us to new insights into divine nature and law, if we pursue the clues. We do not actually integrate with spirit until we find it at the heart of our inquiries and explorations of life.

The best way to start a study of the archetypal nature of beauty, therefore, is to look for how it is expressed in nature, or through the performance of a symphony orchestra, or in the helpful acts of a caring person, and then make an intuitive leap from this physical expression to the essence of beauty in spirit that inspired it. Reading about beauty in a dry philosophic tract may be helpful, but it is no substitute for the actual act of discovery in our mind. A philosopher may inspire us to look, but until we look and see, we remain as ignorant of spirit as we were in the beginning.

Spirit is not an idea; it is much more than an idea. It is a force that embraces the whole of our awareness when we contact it. It inspires us, consoles us, exalts us, and motivates us to utilize what we have learned.

In order to learn about the spiritual dynamics of courage, therefore, we need to observe acts of heroism and sacrifice in times of crisis, and let their inner spiritual nature lift us up to new understanding. The best way to learn about charity is to admire the deeds of people who have dedicated their lives to helping others, such as those doctors who spend their vacations treating the ill and lame in underdeveloped countries. The best way to learn about self-discipline is to observe parents who choose to care for a severely retarded child at home—or an elderly parent with Alzheimer's disease.

In addition to examining people who are successfully expressing spiritual forces in their lives, we must also investigate good and bad examples of action and behavior within ourself and those close to us. We should review, for example, our successes and failures in life. Have our successes served the ideals and intent of spirit? Were our supposed failings significant steps backward—or did they in fact help us learn something valuable about our spiritual agenda? Did our successes teach us useful lessons—or did they strengthen undesirable habits that distract us from our real work? What is the higher perspective of spirit toward our successes and failures?

What does this insight teach us about our inner design? How can we best incorporate this new understanding into our daily activities and behavior—into our spiritual expression?

Just so, we should look at how other people we know embody long-term patterns. Dishonest people usually come to painful ends. This pattern may not be observable immediately, but it will almost certainly arise eventually. Divine law responds to dishonesty with limiting circumstances, loss of friends and support, and perhaps even crippling illnesses. We need to see these patterns and comprehend the workings of law at inner levels. In the same way, a person who always seems to land on both feet after weathering a crisis is probably someone who is willing to help others and support the best within them. It is not as difficult to see these patterns as it might appear, if we cultivate the eyes to see and the mind to comprehend.

A third line of inquiry that can be very helpful is to investigate the true causes of illness, accidents, and misfortune. People who contract cancer at the age of 55 may well have been "setting the table" for the disease through years of resentment, guilt, and negativity. By failing to eliminate these toxins with the forgiving love of spirit, they have created an emptiness in the personality which nurtures the growth of the cancer. Our investigation may also reveal to us that physical treatments of the outer symptoms do not really cure the inner problem. Only the healing forces of spirit can truly cure disease. In this way, we discover the importance of integrating the life of spirit into the attitudes and habits of the personality.

As these investigations unfold—and they need to be approached as open-ended studies—we begin to discover that spirit communicates with us in very subtle whispers and hints, in stark contrast to the blaring cacophony of "conventional wisdom." We therefore always need to exercise great care in insuring that we are properly attuned to the genuine wavelength of spirit, and not the false familiarity of our biases, assumptions, and foolish beliefs.

In truth, the reason why the soul seems to speak to us in whispers is because we are not yet well attuned to it! As we learn to focus on spirit with greater reliability and frequency, the whispers will grow in intensity and clarity. They will still be subtle, but the force of will behind them will become unmistakeable—and unmissable. We will learn to hear even messages that once we might well have rejected.

The second key activity of spiritual integration is **introspection**. As we investigate the inner dimensions to our observations of physical plane life, we must digest our conclusions and convert them into spiritual insights. We must then use these new insights and understandings to revamp and update our beliefs, values, and character.

This process of introspection often requires us to adopt wholly new methodologies—perhaps even new structures of thinking. We disprove earlier assumptions. We move from guessing and surmising to knowing, from what we have read in books to what we have learned through our own skills of observation. We may also move from a theoretical stance to a practical posture. We learn the power of asking the right questions about the events of life—the questions our spiritual nature has been prompting us to ask. Eventually, we learn to frame the key issues of life in the context of spirit, rather than the physical world.

We might, for example, reflect on the plight of a friend who is discovering a terrible void in his thinking—an abyss he has filled with a Hollywoodish concept of life. While our friend is busy deciding which one of his parents deserves a new round of his anger and blame, we may discern that his real problem is spiritual emptiness. He is well-schooled in "vanity fair" kinds of manners, but has no substance. As long as he continues in this way, he dooms himself to be miserable and empty, even though a dollop of wisdom or common sense would transform his life dramatically.

By observing such problems in others, we can trigger important insights in our own thinking, reminding ourself that the substance of life is found entirely in spirit, not in the transitory phenomena of daily life. We may therefore be inspired to accelerate our daily attunement to spirit, and redouble our efforts to integrate its qualities into our own self-expression.

The same process of introspection can help us tap an ever greater measure of spirit if we use it to review and digest the meaning of our creative triumphs. It can help us comprehend what factors and forces helped us excel—and how we can apply them successfully in other circumstances. A mother arriving home from work may be besieged by her children, interfering with other chores and the preparation of dinner. Such a person needs to employ her skills in managing employees at work to managing the demands on her time at home. By spending 15 to 20 minutes focusing first on the needs of the kids, who have been waiting all day to see her, it becomes possible to clear out the time needed to attend to other activities.

God does not rake the leaves. We have chores and duties that only we can perform; spirit cannot do them for us. The lesson to learn is that we can do them twice as well if we do them in the company of spirit. Faith is not enough. Faith helps us become aware of the presence of spirit in our life. But once we have learned this lesson, we must add skill, love, and wisdom to our faith. The work of introspection helps make this transformation possible.

The third and final stage of spiritual integration is **investiture**. Having extracted spiritual meaning and wisdom from our observations through introspection, we must find ways to apply these insights into our expression of who we are and how we live. We must invest spirit into our daily life.

We do not understand a divine archetype fully until we are able to express it without distortion in our daily labors and relationships. It may be nice to tap the spiritual force of joy and let it exalt us during a peak moment

166

of meditation. But we do not truly "own" joy until we are able to act cheerfully in the face of bitter opposition and harsh obstacles. The same principle applies to all of the treasures of spirit. Divine strength is meaningless to us unless we are able to convert it to courage in the face of danger.

In fact, we cannot claim intimate knowledge of any spiritual force until we have demonstrated our ability to express it in times of fatigue, great stress, and challenge. The control of spirit over the personality is never assessed in terms of how we behave when all is going well. It is tested in moments when the very fabric of life seems to be unraveling. Are we able to act as spirit has designed us to act in such moments—or do we fall back on automatic habits of defensiveness, anger, and blame?

The keys to the work of investiture are duty and dedication. It is our primary duty as a human being to learn as much as we can from the lessons and karma of our life. For an agent of light, it is likewise a duty to approach every circumstance of life as though we are imbued with spirit. We are obliged to put the strengths of spirit that we honestly possess to work in the best way possible.

The agent of light does not seek to minimize the scope of duty. On the contrary, he seeks to expand it. He sees a duty to help, advise, teach, and support the people who cross his path in this life. He likewise sees a duty to community—not to remold it to fit some ideological model, but to help reveal its highest potential. And he see a duty to God, by forthrightly taking stands on the major issues facing humanity and society. He labors to evoke a more enlightened response from the mass of mankind.

Dedication is the perfect mate to duty. Through dedication, we strengthen the connection we have made with spiritual purpose. We see in our own life opportunities by which we can fulfill this purpose and serve it needs. It is our dedication that empowers us to get the right things done—even in the face of opposition and attack.

For the purpose of practicing this lesson in spiritual integration, we should select one spiritual quality or force to examine. It could be joy or harmony or beauty or strength. In order to illustrate how to put this lesson to work, we will select "steadfastness."

The work of investigation begins as we honestly ask: do we fully understand the spiritual nature of steadfastness? Do we perceive how greater endurance would enhance our creative work—and alter our values and priorities? Or do we still confuse steadfastness with stubbornness and stagnation?

Once we have settled on a spiritual definition of steadfastness, we can begin the work of introspection. Are we steadfast in spiritual observances—or are we constant only in foolishness or vanity? Are we able to see the opportunities within our problems—or do we lash out instead defensively, trying to defeat our opposition, rather than redeem it?

A second line of introspection is also important. Have we linked our expression of steadfastness with its spiritual origins? Or do we give up and yield at the first signs of discomfiture?

This review is then concluded by the investiture of our new insights into our daily activities. Where can we apply a greater measure of steadfastness? In losing weight? In helping a child cope with a difficult problem? Or in dealing with bosses at work who often seem to act in bewildering and perhaps inhuman ways?

Once we have chosen a primary activity in which we need more steadfastness, we must then work diligently to install this spiritual treasure in our own enlightened self-expression.

14.

Integrating with Groups

Individuality is one of the primary hallmarks of human life and development. But as we tread the spiritual path, we begin to discover how limited one individual can be. Our very own sphere of abilities and opportunities restricts our capacity to help, serve, and lead. In an odd way, the closer we come to harnessing our full potential and power as a human, the more poignantly we realize the limits of our individuality, and how we cannot progress further on our own. We must start looking beyond ourself to form alliances with the groups of people, visible and invisible alike, who can help us serve and lead—in a much broader sphere and scope than before.

The growth of the importance of organized groups in human society over the last few centuries parallels the need of the agent of light to recognize and integrate with the spiritual groups that stand ready to embrace and support him.   Two hundred years ago, humans worked more or less independently, running a family farm or working in a cottage industry.   As society continued to evolve, people started leaving the farm and joining forces with one another in factories and associations and foundations.

As a result, we have learned that by forming groups of similarly-talented individuals, we can greatly increase the productivity, growth, efficiency, and development of every single person. Twenty thousand people working independently would be unable to fly a single jet airliner.   But the coordinated and collective effort of twenty thousand people working together *can* fly planes, succcessfully transporting hundreds of thousands of people every day.

We are not always aware of belonging to such groups. A carpenter may still be his own boss, but be hired as a subcontractor to help frame a house. He becomes part of a group temporarily, while the work progresses. And to the degree that he keeps himself up-to-date on the styles, methods, and requirements of his trade, he aligns himself with the very large group of the "construction trade." In fact, he is also part of an even larger, although abstract group: the invisible group that inspires efficient and esthetic design in home and commercial construction.

In much the same way, an "at-home" mother is a part of a vast group, even though she works on her own and seldom leaves her neighborhood. She is part of the network of people who nurture healing and growth in humanity.

Such groups form the inner—i.e., unseen—structure of human civilization. Collectively, they inspire trends and developments in physical life, in the person as well as in society, even though most people are unaware of them and seemingly nonresponsive to them. In actual fact, we respond to these groups even if we have no conscious understanding that we do.

Obviously, the more we can become aware of them and integrate with their purposes and plans, the more we elevate and enrich the work we do. The duties of motherhood, for instance, have been greatly facilitated by the intense focus of psychology, medicine, and education in developing more effective programs and methods for child rearing. Every mother today knows vastly more than fifty years ago about detecting and dealing with signs of difficulty in young children.

We often take such advances for granted. It can therefore be quite instructive and enlightening to study these developments and appreciate how they have elevated the work of the individual and redefined it in terms of the growth of civiliziation.

The carpenter of today is able to work much more quickly than fifty years ago, thanks to staple guns, better insulating products, treated lumber, and more effective glues and resins. He can therefore be much more productive than before while building superior products.

In a very real sense, the individual carpenter is working side by side with thousands of people who were involved in inventing and producing the tools and products he uses. Many of these people may have been working in entirely different industries or professions—in the space program or computer research. But if their discoveries and work lead to a better product for the carpenter, they become part of his group—and he becomes part of theirs.

Every human being is connected to these larger groups, both visible and invisible, by being part of the human race. There are seven major groups within humanity, each one inspiring and guiding its own phase of human culture: education, the arts, science, government, commerce, the healing arts and sciences, and spirituality. [We referred to these groups as "workshops" in the fifth volume of The Life of Spirit, *The Divine Workshop.*]

Even people who attack big business or government or religion are linked by their acts to these inner groups! The stronger their protest or attack may be, the stronger their tie—and responsibility to act wisely—becomes. After all, the law of cause and effect does not allow protests and attacks to go unanswered indefinitely. They create a debt that must eventually be repaid. Such protestors should ponder on the fact that big business is the very force that feeds them, clothes them, educates them, and gives them the money to fly to the next demonstration!

The claim that these unseen groups do not exist does not diminish them or their influence in any way. It just creates a cloud of darkness around the person making the claim. As an agent of light, we need to expand our vision to recognize these groups. We need to appreciate the immense inspiration, power, and support we can derive from them. We also need to work consciously to integrate our own efforts and thoughts more completely with the direction and guidance of the invisible groups that resonate with our life and activities.

As this integration occurs, we gain a deeper appreciation of the activities that engage us. We acquire a sense of affinity, leading to a deeper fellowship with others involved in the same activities, be they parents, carpenters, journalists, or teachers.

More importantly, we begin to recognize a deeper purpose in our work. If a carpenter, we are not just pounding nails; we are building habitats. If a parent, we are rearing the next generation of society. We are laboring in the earthly garden of God. We are making our contribution to the grand plan.

This link with a larger purpose brings to us a fresh measure of the spiritual power to act effectively.

The need to integrate with the invisible groups of mankind emphasizes one of the most basic choices we must make: how do we choose to live in this world? Do we approach life with a core of noble aspiration and hope, eager to help where we can? Or do we approach it with gloom, anger, anxiety, and intense self-absorption?

It is extremely easy to slip into a reactive mode in our approach to humanity. A support group might form to help people cope with a chronic disease, but lose its focus on overcoming the illness and deteriorate into a weekly gripe session. Not only does this shift in focus make it impossible to overcome the disease, but it also separates us from the qualities and resources that might be able to help!

As we descend into progressively more narrow and selfish concerns, we alienate ourself from the potential help of spirit. We betray our spiritual purpose. When this occurs on a large scale, it produces lots of small "cells" of people complaining about their suffering and misery and blaming the rest of humanity for their ills. They end up placing their problems above all others, and demand that they be solved first.

At its worst, this choice produces factionalism: my group above all others. Examples of such groups would be ecoterrorists who believe it is okay to burn down a ski lodge in order to save the environment; radical socialists who attack capitalism in order "to improve the quality of life for all," even though capitalism already has been hugely successful in improving the quality of life; men-hating feminists, who discriminate against men in order to "free" women; the mavens of political correctness, who promote massive intolerance to avoid offending small groups of people; and malcontent theologians who profess to bring us into the presence of God's love by pounding us into submission with guilt, superstition, and threats.

In each of these cases, a wrong focus has reduced these groups to divisive factions rather than smoothly functioning—or even enlightened—associations. They betray their stated purpose, instead of fulfilling it. They encourage the alienation of their members from other groups—and from the spiritual influences that are trying to inspire humanity.

In stark contrast, the genuine spiritual approach to life always draws people together and leads to groups united by shared goals, work, and success. Instead of obsessing on our problems and deficiencies, the group serves as a focus for the inclusive power of spiritual love. It draws us to higher levels of awareness and releases new potential for ongoing growth. It creates a more noble vision of human and divine possibilities.

Such groups are united by shared hope and noble aspirations, even if they never sponsor conventions in Las Vegas. Every parent wants the very best for his or her children. Every citizen wants the best in government. When groups persistently focus on the best they can attain, and follow this intent with creative action, they end up radically different from the groups that emphasize the fear and gloom of selfish interests.

The goal of selfish-interest groups is to get others to solve their problem for them. The goal of a healthy group is to propel humanity forward. The methods of selfish-interest groups highlight fear, guilt, blame, and pessimism. The methods of healthy groups are inspired by the wisdom, love, and hope of spirit. They emphasize self-reliance, even while promoting awareness of the group! The members of the group are expected to solve their own problems through their own acts—drawing on the resources of the groups when needed, of course, but never becoming a burden on the group. Healthy groups use this approach to draw their members out of the morass of exploitation and greed found in selfish-interest groups.

They likewise enrich the life and activities of each individual. Rather than stirring up mischief and antagonism toward others, they constantly renew the hope and optimism of their members. They magnify the opportunities for each person to improve and point them in the right direction. Rather than depressing everyone by focusing on what is wrong, they connect their members to divine purpose and strengthen the tie to the ideal.

As we come to understand the inner dimensions of groups, we may decide it is time to drop our association with some of the outer organizations. In some cases, the choice will be obvious. But in others, it is important to proceed with caution. If we are part of a group because it serves the plan of the soul, it would be a terrible mistake to drop out of it. And so, even if we disagree with some aspects of our church or government, we can opt to strengthen our tie with its inner purpose, instead of severing it. We may suspect that the group is doing a poor job expressing this purpose, but we must also make sure that we do not dishonor it in our passion to leave.

The spiritual person, for example, would reaffirm that our government acts well enough on the whole, even though there may be specific areas of corruption or bureaucracy that do not honor the full potential of the nation. Instead of giving up on our country, we stay focused in hope and optimism, invoking reform and improvements, rather than wallowing in condemnation and scorn.

In this regard, we can recall the example of Socrates, who accepted the death sentence of his peers, even though he knew that the charges against him were false and that the trial was corrupt. When asked why he did not appeal, he replied that having prospered under the laws of Athens for all of his life, he was not about to demand special exemption from them, merely because his life was on the line. He insisted that the law be fulfilled.

To integrate with the important groups of our life, we must carefully review and examine all of our ties. In this way, we can distinguish which groups are helpful to us and our work and which groups are acting against their own higher purpose. Some of the questions to pose in this review might include:

• How well do the acts of the outer group agree with its stated purposes? Are our unions promoting the beliefs of its members—or the conceits of the labor bosses? Are schools teaching children, or are they promoting an agenda that brainwashes students?

• Does the group unite or divide? Does it use blackmail and intimidation to win? Does it protest loudly without making constructive suggestions? Does it advocate programs that actually hurt some people while they help their members? Does it expect everyone else to make all the concessions? Does it rationalize or embrace acts of violence? Does it betray its own purposes in the name of political expediency and power?

• Does the group exhibit arrogant elitism? Does it assume that only it knows what is right or wrong for its members—and for others as well? Does it routinely demonize everyone who dares oppose it? Does it consider the truth to be "hate speech"?

As we reject the dark alleys that lead to divisiveness, and begin to tread the highway of noble aspirations and hope, we gradually become aware of the spiritual well-springs of benevolence and power that are available to enrich the work of any worthwhile group. The work of integration begins as we learn to love this purpose and be guided and directed by it in our actions.

In other words, instead of emphasizing our personal selfish needs, we learn to unite with others in a collective effort to solve all of our problems. We do not selfishly demand that ours be solved first; we crack the eggshell of self-centeredness that has held us captive for so long and begin to discover the active principle of sharing. We attune ourself to the benevolent love and power of spirit.

To this love of purpose, we must add a strong measure of dedication. It is not enough for a mother to know that there is a higher purpose guiding her; it is equally important that she serve this purpose in her acts of parenting. Optimism can be easily shattered by distressing events. It is an unwavering dedication to the highest goals and the best of all possibilities that protects us from succumbing to selfishness or anger when obstacles arise.

As we integrate with the purpose of a group in this way, our understanding of identity expands. We discover that we are something more than just an individual who can gripe and complain and grab for what he wants. We realize we are even something more than a person who can hold his own competitively or defensively against all others. We are an agent of light who can play a significant role in the unfolding drama of civilization.

Through the groups we belong to, we can expand the contributions we can make:

- We can contribute through our profession or work.
- We can contribute through parenting.
- We can contribute through our love of culture.
- We can contribute through our community, state, and nation.

At the same time, our world view will undergo a decided enrichment. We will rise above the use of fear and intimidation in dealing with others; we will recognize the noble possibilities in people. We will be motivated more by benevolence than selfishness, more by helpfulness than by need.

A mother, for example, might realize that she is not just shoveling down cereal and changing diapers; she is providing a wholesome environment in which her children can build strong characters. This kind of realization enriches even the most mundane aspects of parenting—or work or duty or the call to sacrifice. Instead of focusing on irritability, tedium, or the unpleasantness of what we must do, we focus instead on the value of our accomplishment and our own fulfillment. Our efforts and actions are not wasted effort. They help us attain a whole new level of understanding.

In essence, we are discovering and highlighting the spiritual roots of our mundane activities. We learn that we are connected with the divine plan, working through the whole of the human race. This realization adds a new level of meaning and significance to everything that we do.

When we eventually learn to tap the core of purpose in any activity, we will discover something else as well. It is a tie that links us to the inner beings of all other humans as well. And more than that, it connects us with the full scope of human culture, past, present, and future.

With Paul, we come to realize that we are all members of one body, and that body is the Christ. Some of us serve as fingers, some as toes. We have individualized, specialized roles. But the body as a whole is one. And this one body we call humanity works best when all of its many parts function collectively to serve the One common purpose and goal.

This is the Christ within us, our hope of glory.

To work with these ideas, we can focus on one of our primary duties in this life. We should then ask: what noble purpose underlies this duty—not just for us, but for all who share this duty?

Once this purpose is defined, then we should inquire: how should I view my work as I strive to fulfill this purpose? Am I defensive about my work, complaining about all the people and forces conspiring to deny me this chance to contribute? Or am I attuned to the meaning and purpose of this activity and view it as an opportunity for expanding the scope of my influence?

How does this new view enrich my understanding and attitudes—for example, by lifting me out of the irritations of this work? Can I derive endurance from it when obstacles start to overwhelm me? What is the real contribution I am making?

What is the level of my dedication? Does it disappear whenever I am fatiguted or discouraged? Or does it prompt me to strengthen my inner connections and refresh my activity?

How does this review help me become more aware of the larger group with whom I share this labor in God's garden of earth? How does this help me integrate more fully into God's Plan for humanity?

ENLIGHTENMENT

Embracing The Light is a compilation of 14 lessons on the process of spiritual integration from the *Enlightenment* series written by Robert R. Leichtman, M.D. and Carl Japikse and published by Ariel Press.

In addition to this topic, *Enlightenment* deals with six other areas of life. Each has or will become a book:

• *The Revelation of Light,* an exploration of the psychic dimensions of life and how they affect us. In print.

• *The Light of Learning,* which explores the principles of personal and spiritual growth. In print.

• *The Lights of Heaven,* which explores the divine archetypes from which Creation is built. In print.

• *Embodying the Light,* a guide to enlightened self-expression and how it can enrich our lives. 2007.

• *The Light Which Penetrates,* which deals with enriching the human mind. 2009.

• *Our Companions in the Light* examines how other forms of life enrich our own. 2010.

The books cost $14.99 apiece, plus $6 shipping. All 7 may be ordered as a set for $90. The last three books will be sent as they are issued.

It is also possible to subscribe to the lessons as they are written. A new lesson is produced every two months and is sent to subscribers by first-class mail as they are ready. A subscription to one year (six) lessons is $21 postpaid. The cost of subscribing to all 96 lessons is $210.

To order, send a check to Ariel Press, Box 297, Marble Hill, GA 30148. Or email us at sales@lightariel.com.

OTHER BOOKS FROM ARIEL PRESS

ACTIVE MEDITATION
By Robert R. Leichtman, M.D. & Carl Japikse, $26.99

THE ART OF LIVING
A five-volume set of essays
By Robert R. Leichtman, M.D. & Carl Japikse, $55

THE LIFE OF SPIRIT
A five-volume set of essays
By Robert R. Leichtman, M.D. & Carl Japikse, $60

FEAR NO EVIL
By Robert R. Leichtman, M.D., $9.95

THE CURSE OF FUNDAMENTALISM
by Robert R. Leichtman, M.D., $14.99

THE STORY OF GOD
by Carl Japikse, $17.99

THE LIGHT WITHIN US
by Carl Japikse, $10.95

PRACTICAL MYSTICISM
by Evelyn Underhill, $13.99

THE GIFT OF HEALING
by Ambrose & Olga Worrall, $14.99